Travel Guide for the Dutch Flower Region
Copyright © 2018 Bollenstreek Reisgids
Voorhout, First Edition, March 2018
Author: Marti van Beek

Printed by: Pumbo.nl
Publisher: Bollenstreek Reisgids
Design: Denise van Starkenburg - www.denisevanstarkenburg.nl

Photographs:

Marti van Beek - www.bollenstreek-reisgids.nl
(All photographs except for the ones specified below)
FAM Flower Farm - www.famflowerfarm.nl - coverfoto
Dirk van Egmond - www.treffendbeeld.nl
p.30, p.32, p.33, p.34, p.35, p.37, p..46/47, p.50/51,
p.53, p.54, p.57, p.81, p.122, p.154, p.161
Purple_Owlie - instagram - Photo p.70
Bernadette Schoone - www.bernadetteschoone7.wixsite.com/mijnsite
Photos on p.58/59, p.63, p.64, p.143 top
Jeanette van Starkenburg - www.jeanettevanstarkenburg.nl
Photos on p.73, p.78, p.79, p.99 bottom, p.129)
Marjolein van Veldhuizen & Jordy Stuivenberg - www.weblendit.nl
(p.2 /3, p.8, p.20/21, p.74/75)

www.bollenstreek-reisgids.nl / info@bollenstreek-reisgids.nl

ISBN nummer: 978-90-828388-0-0

SpecialthankstoCorinevanBeek,AnnePennekamp,DenisevanStarkenburgandMikeCox.

Travel Guide
for the Dutch Flower Region

MartivanBeek

INDEX

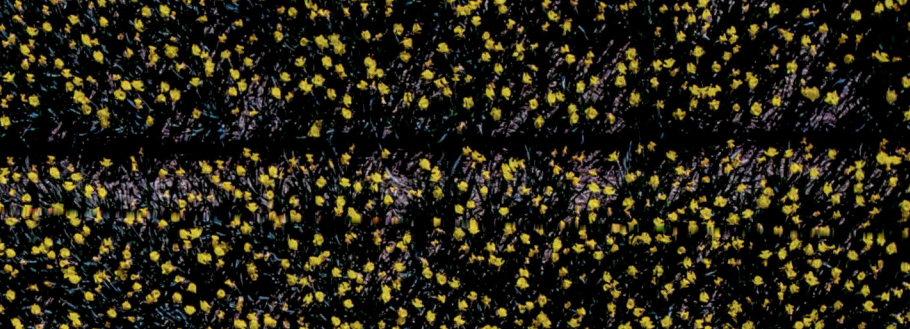

Introduction
to the Dutch Flower Region

5 Golf courses, 9 Theaters, 12 Marinas, 13 Museums, 21 Galleries, more than 100 Hotels, Bed & Breakfasts and Campsites and more than 260 Restaurants…
… and 2 Indoor ski slopes, 2 Bowling alleys, 4 Casinos, 6 Wellness centres, 7 Swimming pools, 33 Beach pavilions, the Beach of Katwijk, the Beach of Noordwijk, beautiful Parks, the Kagerplassen, Forests, Dunes, Keukenhof, and in spring hundreds of thousands, or perhaps even millions of hyacinths, daffodils and tulips that show the region at its best and most colourful side.

You can find it all in the Dutch Flower Region (in Dutch: Bollenstreek), at less than half an hour away from Amsterdam, capital of the Netherlands. This guide will help you on your way to find everything you need to enjoy a pleasant stay in the Dutch Flower Region. The 6 municipalities of the Flower Region include 11 villages (including De Zilk), each with its own character, its own landscapes and also its peculiarities.

This travel guide enables you to easily find dozens of addresses for the type of overnight stay that suits you best. From campsites and small B&B addresses to luxury 5 star hotels. Furthermore, you will find an overview of all restaurants in each village. If you want to go out for dinner, you will easily find a nice restaurant nearby. Besides these places to stay and places to eat you will find all the sights worth visiting and an extensive list of activities, from playgrounds to helicopter flights. All this to make your stay a truly unforgettable adventure.

Marti van Beek - Author

Wishing you a very pleasant stay in the Dutch Flower Region.

Practical details

Public transport

From Schiphol Airport you can reach the Flower Region by train, bus or taxi within half an hour. From NS Station Schiphol Airport, a Sprinter train goes to The Hague. This stops at Sassenheim station and Leiden station. From Leiden you will be in Voorhout station (take the Sprinter train towards Haarlem) in five minutes. Bus line 50 from Leiden to Haarlem stops, among other places, in Warmond, Sassenheim, Lisse and Hillegom. Bus line 30 takes you from Leiden to Katwijk. And line 20 goes from Leiden to Noordwijk. From Voorhout station, bus line 57 goes to Noordwijkerhout.

The train stations and the extensive bus network make for a well-accessible Flower Region. The villages Hillegom, Sassenheim and Voorhout have a train station. Within half an hour you will be in the Amsterdam city centre, The Hague or Haarlem. Leiden only takes about five minutes by train from Voorhout station or Sassenheim station. To plan your trip, you can use the travel planner for train, tram, bus and subway: www.9292.nl/en

Taxis

At Schiphol Airport there is a wide range of taxi companies that can bring you to the Flower Region. A single trip by taxi from Schiphol to, for example, Noordwijk costs about 50 Euros. There are many illegal taxis at Schiphol Airport. Avoid these! Insurance, prices and driver identity are unclear and the ride may not be safe. Therefore, always take an official taxi. Official taxis can be identified by a blue license plate and / or a roof light and they drive on the taximeter. Official taxi companies that can take you to the Flower Region:

AC Taxi - 24/7 Schiphol service
Tel. 071 - 362 50 22 www.actaxiservice.nl

Taxi Bollenstreek - 24/7 Schiphol service
Tel. 0252 - 508 888 www.taxibollenstreek.nl

Schiphol Taxi - 24/7 Schiphol service
Tel. 071 - 887 38 88 www.noordwijktaxicentrale.nl

Travelling around

An excellent way to discover the Flower Region is by bike, Vespa or Solex, Renault Twizy or even a helicopter (see Activities for rental companies). Enjoy the old-Dutch landscape, the mills, the characteristic villages and the beautiful flower fields. Bicycle routes are available on www.bollenstreek-reisgids.nl (see section Activities) or at the various Tourism offices (in Dutch: VVV) in the Flower Region.

Tourism Offices

VVV Katwijk
Koningin Wilhelminastraat 9 - 2225 AZ Katwijk aan Zee Tel. 071 - 407 54 44

VVV Lisse
Heereweg 219 - 2161 BG Lisse Tel. 0252 - 417 900

VVV Noordwijk
Jan Kroonsplein 4 - 2202 JC Noordwijk Tel. 071 - 361 93 21

VVV Noordwijkerhout
Dorpsstraat 8 - 2211 GC Noordwijkerhout Tel. 0252 - 372 096

VVV Warmond
Gemeentehaven 3 - 2361 CM Warmond Tel. 071 - 301 06 31

Shopping

Lisse shopping centre

With more than 130 stores, Lisse has the largest retail offer in the Flower region. Most of the major brands have a shop next to nice little boutiques. From clothes to toy stores and from electronics to bookstores. Most shops are located in and around the Kanaalstraat. Parking is free. On Monday morning most stores are closed. On Thursday evening, it's shopping evening, and only on shopping Sundays are the shops open on Sundays.

Shopping in Hillegom

Hillegom shopping centre is characterised by the presence of cosy catering industry and more than 100 original specialty stores. The weekly market is on Tuesdays between 8 and 17 hours on Henri Dunantplein. There is ample parking space near the shopping centre and parking is free.

Shop till you drop in Noordwijk

You can shop in both the historic centre of Noordwijk-Binnen and in the Hoofdstraat in Noordwijk aan Zee. Especially in the Hoofdstraat there are many fashion stores, even for the latest bathing suit fashion you are at the right place here. If you have had enough of all the shopping, there are plenty of restaurants available near the shopping street for a refreshing cup of coffee or a delicious lunch. In Noordwijk aan Zee the shops are also open on Sundays. The other villages in the Flower Region have nice authentic shopping streets just like Lisse, Hillegom and Noordwijk worth visiting just as well.

Nightlife

Except for the local bars that you will find in every village, nightlife of the Dutch Flower Region is mainly concentrated on De Grent in Noordwijk. This is the perfect place for a good night out with a variety of bars and nightclubs. In weekends bars and clubs in Noordwijk close at 4.00 am. Smoking and the use of drugs is forbidden in all bars and clubs and the minimum legal drinking age is 18 years. Identification may be asked for.

Bar Dancing The Champ
De Grent 20 - 2202 EL Noordwijk www.thechamp.nl

Home Noordwijk
De Grent 14 - 2202 EL Noordwijk www.home-noordwijk.nl

Het Koffiehuis
De Grent 32 - 2202 EL Noordwijk www.hetkoffiehuis.nl

Open Doors
De Grent 34 - 2202 EL Noordwijk www.open-doors.nl

Cafe Rosser
De Grent 10 - 2202 EL Noordwijk www.caferosser.nl

Zeepaardje
De Grent 16-18 - 2202 EL Noordwijk www.zeepaardje.nl

Banks&Emergency

Banks and currency

In every village you will find bank offices that are usually open between 9 am and 5 pm. Rabobank, ABN AMRO, ING Bank and SNS are typical Dutch banks that have offices in most places. You will easily find ATM's of one of these banks in the shopping centres. In most stores you will be able to pay by creditcard as well. Like most of Europe the euro is used as form of currency in The Netherlands.

Emergency numbers

Police, Ambulance, Fire:	112
National Police (non-emergency)	0900 - 8844
Hospital / First Aid	071 - 526 91 11
Leiden University Medical Center	
Albinusdreef 2 - 2333 ZA Leiden	
Medical center / First Aid	0252 - 240 212
Huisartsenpost Duin- en Bollenstreek	
Rijnsburgerweg 4-B - 2215 RA Voorhout	

Holidays&Climate

National Holidays in The Netherlands

January 1 - New Year's Day

Good Friday - the Friday before Easter (not an official public holiday)

Easter Sunday - always between 22nd March and 25th April

Easter Monday - Monday after Easter Sunday

April 27 - **King's Birthday**

If 27th is a Sunday, celebrations are held on 26th

May 4 - National Remembrance Day (not an official public holiday)

May 5 - Liberation Day (official public holiday every 5 years, next in 2020)

Ascension Day - 40 days after Easter

Pentecost Sunday - 50 days after Easter

Pentecost Monday - Monday after Easter Sunday

December 5 - Sinterklaas

(traditional Dutch holiday, not an official public holiday)

December 25 - Christmas Day

December 26 - Boxing Day

Special events in the Dutch Flower Region

Carnival - 3 days before Ash Wednesday (40 days before Easter)

Flower Parade - 'Bloemencorso van de Bollenstreek'

annually on the first Saturday after April 19

Flower Parade Rijnsburg - annually on the second Saturday of August

Climate

The Netherlands have a temperate maritime climate influenced by the North Sea and Atlantic Ocean, with cool summers and moderate winters. Average daytime temperatures vary from 2°C-6°C in the winter and 17°C-20°C in the summer.

Since the country is small there is little variation in climate from region to region, although the marine influences are less inland. Rainfall is distributed throughout the year with a dryer period from April to September.

THE FLOWER PARADE is about to set out on the streets from Noordwijk to Haarlem, **in full bloom!**

When to visit

The Dutch Flower Region has its charms all year round. Bear in mind that if you want to see the flowers bloom in Keukenhof and all the flowerfields surrounding it, you will have to plan your trip between mid March and mid May.

Daffodils are the first flowers to bloom in the month of March. In April you will have the best chance to see millions of hyacinths and tulips blooming everywhere in the Flower Region. Although Keukenhof is usually open until mid May, in most fields surrounding it the tulips may have already been harvested at that time. It's the bulb that matters for the farmers, not the flower.

Talking about the flower fields and farmers, please respect the farmers requests not to walk into the flower fields as diseases may be transferred or crop may be damaged. So take your best holiday pictures standing on the edge of the flower fields, not right in the middle of it.

During the rest of the year you will be able to see other beautiful flower fields, like for example dahlia flower fields that bloom in August and September. An excellent tool to see which flowers are blooming at the time you are visiting the Flower Region is the flower radar: www.flowerradar.com

In summertime you can enjoy the beautiful beaches of Katwijk and Noordwijk and have a drink, lunch or dinner, in one of the trendy beach restaurants. Looking for adventure? What about supping, kiting, skimboarding, bodyboarding, wakeboarding or windsurfing! Enjoy beach life big time!

Useful vocabulary

Yes	Ja
No	Nee
Please	Alstublieft
Here you are	Alstublieft
Thank you	Dank u wel
No, thank you	Nee, dank u
You're welcome	Geen dank
Excuse me (getting attention)	Sorry
Do you speak English?	Spreekt u Engels?
I'm sorry (begging pardon)	Sorry
Good	Goed
Okay	Okee
Maybe	Misschien
I don't know	Ik weet het niet
Hi	Hoi
Bye	Doei
Hello	Hallo
Good morning	Goedemorgen
Good afternoon	Goedemiddag
Good evening	Goedenavond
Good night	Goedenacht
Goodbye	Tot ziens
See you later	Tot straks
Have a good journey	Goede reis

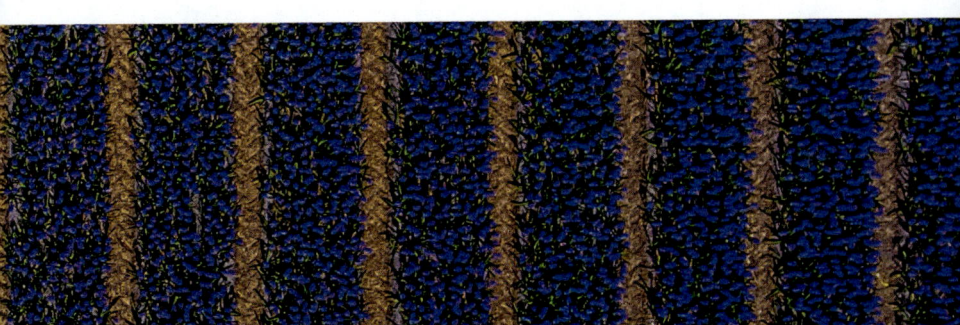

Let's find some
BEAUTIFUL
place to get lost

Hillegom
Village with a rich history

The most northern community of the Flower Region. Hillegom is a village with more than 21,000 inhabitants. Unlike some other villages in the Flower Region, around Hillegom only a small amount of bulb fields have been lost at the expense of residential construction. The name Hillegom is derived from Hilleghem, mentioned in old archives. Heem stands for a place of residence and it is likely that Hille is a bastardization of a personal name like Hildegard or Hildebert. The meaning would then be House of Hille. The village originated in the early Middle Ages around the Maartenskerk (Maartsen's Church), the Houttuin and the Court of Hillegom (Hof van Hillegom).

The people from Hillegom (Hillegommers) initially engaged in agriculture and livestock farming. In the 17th and 18th centuries, vegetables, fruit and herbs began to be cultivated and daily barges moved to the markets in Leiden and Amsterdam. During this time, also beautiful outside places (buitenplaatsen) were founded in Hillegom. Unfortunately, these have been in decay over time and eventually demolished. From the middle of the 19th century, flower bulb cultivation has brought a lot of prosperity. The beautiful flower fields around Hillegom and the annual flower parade (bloemencorso) bring many tourists to the village.

In the early years of Dutch television, many recordings were made of shows and performances in the big hall of Treslong. In 1964, The Beatles performed a playback TV show for the VARA. In 2005 the complex was demolished and the new residential area 'De Marel' was built on site.

1

1- 't Klokgeveltje, Hoofdstraat 140, Hillegom

The Klokgeveltje is one of the oldest houses in Hillegom. On the fine facade stands 1794, but the premise was already there in 1634. In the house lived and worked beer traders, bakers, butchers and florists. Since 1975 it is again a residential home. The basement below the building on the right is part of the Klokgeveltje.

2 - Hof van Hillegom, Hoofdstraat 115, Hillegom

In the heart of Hillegom opposite the Maartenskerk lies the Court of Hillegom. The Court has a medieval origin; the court was already mentioned in the 14th century. It may have been built in the 10th or 11th century. The Lord of Hillegom, Mr. Jan Six bought it in 1749 and the house remained in the family until 1822. It is the only remaining outside residence in Hillegom. Since 1903 the Court of Hillegom has been used as a town hall.

3 - Houttuin, Hillegom

The Grote Pomp (Big Pump) is a natural stone pump, built in 1740 by Jan Six. This craftsman from Hillegom had made a well on De Houttuin to provide the village with fresh water. The pump was in operation until Hillegom got a water pipe in 1925. In 1983 the pump was restored. The triangular village square where the Queen Wilhelminaboom and the Dorpspomp stand is the Houttuin, probably because the firewood for the village used to be stored here.

4 - Maartenskerk,
Kerkplein 1, Hillegom

At the place where a chapel already stood in 1248, the Maartenskerk was built shortly after. The Maartenskerk is a Protestant church, but was originally the Catholic Sint Maartenskerk. At the bottom of the tower was once the prison of the village of Hillegom. The ship of the church was destroyed around 1575 during the battle between Spaniards and Geuzen. In 1929 the section between the tower and choir was rebuilt. The tower survived a fire in 1978.

4

5 - Sint Jozefkerk,
Monseigneur van Leeuwenlaan, Hillegom

The Saint Joseph's Church was a Roman Catholic church at the Monseigneur van Leeuwenlaan in Hillegom dedicated to Joseph of Nazareth. In 1870/1871 the Sint Martinus church was built after the large clandestine church on the Bakummerlaan had become too small for the many parishioners. Because of the rise of the flower bulb culture, the population of Hillegom grew so hard that in 1915 a second parish was founded and the Sint Jozefkerk was built.

In 1990, both parishes were merged because of the declining church visit. The Sint Jozefkerk was disposed of but the church building is still on the Monseigneur van Leeuwenlaan. Whether the church will be demolished or will get a new destination is still unclear. In 2009, the 'Vereniging Behoud Jozefkerk en Pastorie' (English: Association for the Conservation of the Jozefkerk and Rectory) was created with the aim of preserving the buildings.

6

6 - Sint Martinuskerk, Hoofdstraat 27b, Hillegom

St. Martin's Church is a Roman Catholic church at Hoofdstraat 29 in Hillegom. The church was built in 1870/1871 after the large Clandestine church on the Bakummerlaan had become too small for the many parishioners. Because of the rise of the flower bulb culture, the population of Hillegom grew so hard that in 1915 a second parish was founded and the Sint Jozefkerk was built. Saint Martin's Church quickly became too small and so a new church was built between 1923 and 1926. Due to lack of money, it was decided not to build a new tower, but to integrate the old tower into the new church. In 1990, both parishes were merged because of the declining church visit. The Sint Jozefkerk was disposed of but the church building is still on the Monseigneur van Leeuwenlaan. The Sint Martinuskerk was thoroughly restored and renovated in 2008/2009.

5

WHERE TO STAY
IN HILLEGOM

Hotel

Hotel Villa Flora ★★★
Hoofdstraat 55
2181 EB Hillegom
Tel. 0252 - 515 100
www.hotelvillaflora.nl

Bed & Breakfast

B&B Bij de Zuilen
Zandlaan 18
2181 HS Hillegom
Tel. 06 - 54 97 27 78
www.bedbreakfast.bijdezuilen.nl

B&B Bollenstreek
Prins Hendrikstraat 31
2181 AN Hillegom
Tel. 0252 - 347 310

B&B De Groene Bollenschuur
Leidsestraat 152
2182 DS Hillegom
Tel. 06 - 53 44 78 70
www.degroenebollenschuur.nl

B&B Wilhelmina
Wilhelminalaan 80
2182 CE Hillegom
Tel. 06 - 83 17 00 61

B&B Zuidervaart
Zuider Leidsevaart 4
2182 NC Hillegom
Tel. 0252 - 751 929

zzz..

RESTAURANTS
IN HILLEGOM

Het Alternatief 🇳🇱
Hoofdstraat 29
2181 EA Hillegom
Tel. 0252 - 688 668
www.t-alternatief.nl

BBQ Restaurant Hillegom
Hoofdstraat 164-168
2182 EP Hillegom
Tel. 0252 - 528 471
www.bbqhillegom.nl

Bij Deborah 🇫🇷
Meerstraat 27
2181 BH Hillegom
Tel. 0252 - 523 299
www.restaurantseray.nl

Bistro Seray 🇮🇩
Van den Endelaan 36
2181 EK Hillegom
Tel. 0252 - 865 765
www.restaurantseray.nl

Brasserie de Houttuin
(coffee & lunch)
Houttuin 6
2181 JG Hillegom
Tel. 0252 - 517 071
www.dehouttuin.nl

Da Fratello 🇮🇹
Hoofdstraat 84
2181 EE Hillegom
Tel. 0252 - 543 212
www.dafratello.nl

Eetcafé Zomerzorg 🇳🇱
Meerlaan 70
2181 BT Hillegom
Tel. 0252 - 515 228
www.zomerzorg.nl

Hotel Villa Flora 🇳🇱 🇫🇷
Hoofdstraat 55
2181 EB Hillegom
Tel. 0252 - 515 100
www.hotelvillaflora.nl/
restaurant-hillegom

Lange Muur 🇨🇳
Sixlaan 22
2181 AB Hillegom
Tel. 0252 - 517 270
www.langemuurhillegom.nl

McDonald's Hillegom (Fast food)
Arnoudstraat 5
2182 DZ Hillegom
Tel. 0252 - 530 625
www.mcdonaldsrestaurant.nl/
hillegom

Mikaku 🇯🇵
Haarlemmerstraat 2
2181 HC Hillegom
Tel. 0252 - 532 335
www.mikaku-hillegom.nl

La Rueda 🇦🇷
Molenstraat 4 - 2181 JB Hillegom
Tel. 0252 - 526 688
www.larueda.nl

De Soete Suikerbol
(Pancakes 🇳🇱 & more)
Hoofdstraat 34A
2181 ED Hillegom
Tel. 0252 - 522 287
www.hillegom.suikerbol.nl

Vissen bij de Zuilen 🇳🇱
Zandlaan 18 - 2181 HS Hillegom
Tel. 023 - 584 99 91
www.de-zuilen.nl

You Hachi - All You Can Eat 🇯🇵
Henri Dunantplein 9
2181 EM Hillegom
Tel. 0252 - 530 170
www.youhachi.nl

Dutch cuisine
French cuisine
Indonesian cuisine
Italian cuisine
Spanish cuisine
Chinese cuisine
Japanese cuisine
Argentine cuisine

29

Katwijk, Rijnsburg and Valkenburg ZH

Katwijk - The municipality of Katwijk consists of the five centres Katwijk aan Zee, Katwijk aan den Rijn, Katwijk-Noord, Valkenburg ZH and Rijnsburg, and it is the largest municipality of the Flower Region with a total of more than 62,000 inhabitants. In particular, the fishing village of Katwijk aan Zee has been able to maintain its identity well. The Katwijkse dialect (Katteks / Kattuks) is still spoken and contains many words from ancient Dutch from the seventeenth century and even from the Middle Ages such as skoe and skoe-e (for the Dutch words: schoen and schoenen, which means shoe and shoes in English) and skoere (schouders, which in English means shoulders). The name Katwijk may be derived from the Germanic tribe de Chatten, and wijk (which means: neighborhood) comes from the Latin word vicus, residence. In Roman times, the strategic location of the place was of great importance. The northern border of the Roman Empire lay along the Rhine.

The name Catwijck is seen for the first time in documents from 1231. The municipality of Katwijk dates back to 1817 and shows a blue Andreas cross. St. Andreas has traditionally been the patron saint of fishermen. The current view of the Katwijkse boulevard originates from after the Second World War. During the war, a 200m long strip of houses had to make place for the Atlantikwall (Atlantic wall). In 2006, the municipalities of Valkenburg ZH and Rijnsburg were merged with Katwijk. Over time Katwijk as well as Noordwijk have grown into one of the major tourist attractions of the Dutch coast.

Rijnsburg
- In 2006, Rijnsburg accounted for slightly less than 15,000 inhabitants. The village is especially famous for the Rijnsburgse Flower Parade (Rijnsburgse Bloemencorso) annually on the second Saturday in August and the FloraHolland establishment. It was not until the sixth century that there was a real village. The Frisians had settled there. In an ecclesiastical writing of the year 750, it is spoken of 'Rudolfsheim, now called Rinasburg'. In the year 975, Dirk II won the battle against the West Frisians and founded the Laurentius chapel. In the centre of the 'old' Rijnsburg is the Wilhelminaboom. This tree was planted in 1898 in honor of Princess Wilhelmina's 18th birthday. During the occupation years 1940-1945 the tree was the symbol of opposition to the occupier. In the night of 31 August 1941 (Wilhelmina's birthday) the tree was decorated festively. A group of 30 random Rijnburgers were later arrested and imprisoned in the prison Oranjehotel (Orange Hotel) in Scheveningen. The occupant tried to poison the tree a few days after, but it is still there today. The philosopher Baruch Spinoza lived in Rijnsburg between 1661 and 1663. The Spinoza House (Spinozahuisje) is one of the places of special interest in Rijnsburg. The late mayor of Amsterdam Eberhard van der Laan used to live in Rijnsburg.

Valkenburg ZH
is a small village with about 4,000 inhabitants. The village is mostly known for the naval airport Valkenburg ZH Airport (Vliegveld Valkenburg ZH). In 2006 this airport was closed and since 2010 the musical 'Soldaat van Oranje' (Soldier of Orange) has been performed in the theater hangar. Around the Valkenburg ZH Lake lies a narrow-gauge Railway (smalspoorlijn). From Ascension Day to the last weekend of September, you can take a ride with the steam train around the lake.

1

1 - Andreaskerk, boulevard 109, Katwijk

The Andreaskerk (Protestant) is also called the Oude Kerk or Witte Kerk (Old Church or White Church) and was built in 1461. After the church was destroyed by the Spaniards in 1572, the church was rebuilt around 1640. The church is named after the Apostle Andreas, the patron saint of fishermen. An azure blue Andreas cross on a silver ground is the coat of arms of the municipality of Katwijk. Initially the church had a pointed tower, but after a fierce storm in 1836 it was so damaged that it had to be demolished.

After the Nieuwe Kerk (New Church) was built on the Voorstraat in 1885, the Oude Kerk was sold in 1890 and it served as a ship shed of the Katwijk Shipping Company until 1921. In 1924 the church was put back into use after the renovation. During the Second World War, the Ortskommandant had ordered that not only the houses on the boulevard but also the Andreaskerk should be demolished for the Atlantic Wall. Due to the contractor who only demolished the tower to roof height, the church was saved. The interior had already been brought to safety. In front of the church is a statue of Louis van der Noordaa, the 'Fisher widow with son'.

2 - Dorpskerk, Kerklaan 12, Katwijk a/d Rijn

The village church was built in the 1231. It is therefore one of the oldest churches in the area. The oldest parts, the tower, the centrepiece, and the main choir are the remains of a Roman Catholic chapel with leprozerie (nursing home for lepers). The other parts date from the 15th and 16th century. Originally it was a Catholic church and the first church in Katwijk. The church has been restored many times. In 1891, 1919, 1925, and 1974-1977. The current entrance was built in 1925. In the church is the grave monument to see Maria van Reygersbergh and her husband Willem van Lyere, made by Rombout Verhulst.

2

3 - Koningshof, Kerkstraat 47, Katwijk aan den Rijn

The Koningshof is a U-shaped courtyard built around a courtyard that originally consisted of eight small houses and a main house. The courtyard was designed by architect Viele and built from the legacy of Antonia Jacoba Koning. On the street side, the Koningshof has a beautiful entrance with a gate with the inscription: 'Anno - Koningshof - 1805'. During the restoration in 1973 the houses were merged into five larger ones. The Koningshof is the former Homestead of Carolus Boers.

4 - Nieuwe Kerk, Voorstraat 79, Katwijk

The Nieuwe Kerk in Katwijk is on the Voorstraat, it was built between 1885 and 1887 and is owned by the Reformed Church in Katwijk. Because the Andreaskerk became too small, it was decided to build a new, larger church. The Baroness of Wassenaer van Catwijck laid the first stone. The tower of the church is one of the highest structures in Katwijk at a height of about 51 meters. It is striking that the church has almost no support points, there are no pillars in the church. The organ is after the Laurenskerk in Rotterdam and the Bavokerk in Haarlem the third largest organ in the Netherlands.

5 - Soefitempel, Zuidduinseweg 7, Katwijk

To the south of the boulevard in the dunes of Katwijk lies the Sufi Temple. It is the only universal Sufism temple in the world. Sufism is characterized by an interaction of religious and spiritual influences and provides methods to realize your ideals. Universal Sufism is not a new religion, but wants to provide a meeting place for all people who desire love, harmony and beauty regardless of their faith, race or class.

The temple bears the name Universel Murad Hassil. In addition to worship services and summer schools, concerts (classical music) are also given. In 1969 the construction of the temple began. The temple has a square shape, with a gold-colored dome on the roof. The square represents stability and strength. The translucent dome symbolizes the human heart that, open to the sky, is open to the divine light. The hall in the temple is 13 by 13 meters and can accommodate about 120 visitors.

6 - De Vuurbaak, Vuurbaakplein 11, Katwijk

The lighthouse of Katwijk, the Vuurbaak or also called Vierboet is after the Brandaris (the lighthouse of Terschelling), the oldest lighthouse in the Netherlands. In 1605 the request for construction was submitted to Stadholder Prince Maurits. Only in 1628 approval was granted.

There used to be a grid on the flat roof of the Vuurbaak on which wood was set on fire. Later this became a coal fire and in the 19th century an oil lamp with reflector. Only if ships from their own fleet had sailed out was the fishermen's light ignited. De Vuurbaak has not been in operation since 1913 because no ships have come ashore in Katwijk since then. Bomschuiten (vessels that were used for herring fishing or scrub fishing) were just lying on the beach.

During the First World War the lighthouse was used as a lookout post by the Koninklijke Marine (Royal Dutch Navy). In the Second World War, the Vuurbaak was used as a machine gun post. Since 1968, the lighthouse has been open to the public in the summer months.

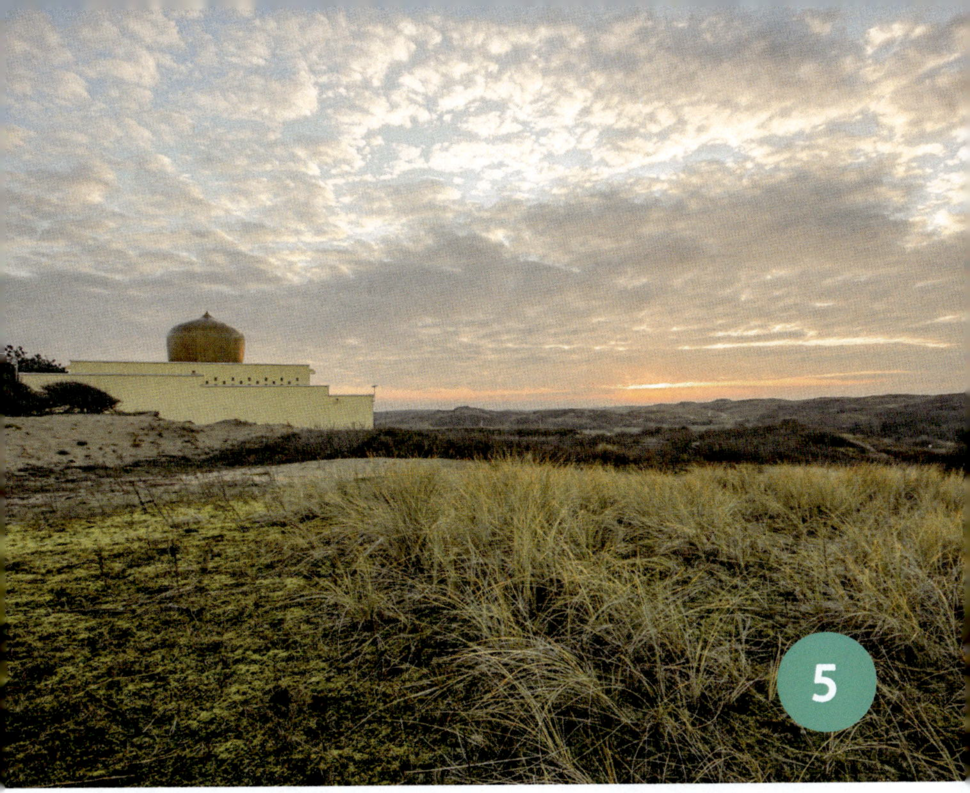

5

6

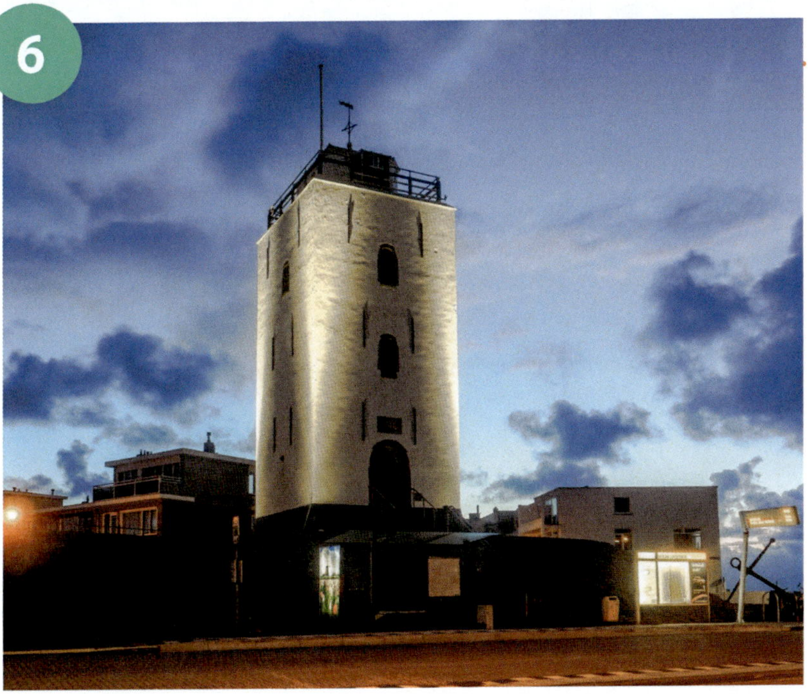

Relax,
life takes time

Zzz..

WHERE TO STAY IN KATWIJK

Hotels

Beachhostel Holland
Badstraat 9
2225 BL Katwijk
Tel. 071 - 240 74 82
www.beachhostelholland.nl

Hotel Noordzee
Boulevard 72
2225 AG Katwijk aan Zee
Tel. 071 - 401 57 42
www.hotelnoordzee.nl

Hotel Seahorse
Boulevard 14
2225 AA Katwijk aan Zee
Tel. 071 - 401 59 21
www.hotelseahorse.nl

Hotel Van Beelen
Koningin Wilhelminastraat 12
2225 BA Katwijk aan Zee
Tel. 071 - 407 33 33
www.hotelvanbeelen.nl

Hotel Zee en Duin
Boulevard 5
2225 AA Katwijk aan Zee
Tel. 071 - 401 33 20
www.zeeenduin.nl

Bed&Breakfast

B&B Aan de Katwijkse kust
Koningin Wilhelminastraat 3
2225 AZ Katwijk
Tel. 071 - 401 46 29
www.katwijksekust.nl

B&B Aan Strand
Boulevard 129 - 2225 HC Katwijk
Tel. 071 - 401 38 90
www.bedandbreakfastaanstrand.nl

B&B Het Oude Dorp
Wassenaarseweg 49
2223 BJ Katwijk
www.hetoudedorpkatwijk.nl
Tel. 06 - 14 64 50 00

B&B In Bos Aan Zee
Nieuwe Duinweg 7
2224 EC Katwijk aan Zee
Tel. 06 - 11 19 68 59
www.inbosaanzee.nl

B&B Katwijk
Andreasplein 4
2225 GR Katwijk
Tel. 071 - 887 31 14
www.bedandbreakfastkatwijk.nl

B&B Kik en Bun
Koningin Wilhelminastraat 4
2225 BA Katwijk aan Zee
Tel. 06 - 10 22 29 42
www.katwijkbedandbreakfast.nl

B&B Locals
Andreasplein 16a
2225 GR Katwijk
Tel. 06 - 49 63 03 22
www.localskatwijk.nl

B&B Mol
Koningin Wilhelminastraat 6
2225 BA Katwijk aan Zee
Tel. 071 - 401 67 10
www.bedandbreakfastmol.nl

Appartments&Holidayhomes

Nicolette Appartementen
Voorstraat 3a
2225 EJ Katwijk aan Zee
Tel. 071 - 401 76 83
www.nicoletteappartementen.nl

Wilma Appartementen
Boulevard 49
2225 AD Katwijk
Tel. 071 - 401 26 85
www.boulevard49.nl

Campings & Bungalows

Vakantiepark Noordduinen
Campingweg 1
2221 EW Katwijk aan Zee
Tel: 071 - 402 52 95
www.noordduinen.nl

Camping De Zuidduinen
Zuidduinseweg 1
2225 JS Katwijk aan Zee
Tel. 071 - 401 47 50
www.zuidduinen.com

Beach Houses

**Strandvakantiehuisjes /
Strandpaviljoen Paal 14**
Boulevard Zeezijde 7
2225 BB Katwijk
Tel. 071 - 401 44 64
www.strandvakantiehuisjeskatwijk.nl

Strandhuisjes Key West Boulevard
Zeezijde 11 / Opposite of Boulevard 50
2225 BB Katwijk aan Zee
Tel. 071 - 401 25 83
www.strandhuisjeskeywest.nl

Kusthuisjes Boulevard
Zeezijde 21/23 - 2225 BB Katwijk aan Zee
Tel. 071 - 401 20 48
www.kusthuisjes.nl

KUST strandhuisjes
Boulevard Zeezijde 41 -
Opposite of Boulevard 141
2225 HD Katwijk aan Zee
Tel. 06 - 83 56 39 42
www.kust.nu

Logeren aan Zee
Strandvak 22 Noordduinseweg
2221 BL Katwijk
Tel. 071 - 408 23 80
www.logerenaanzee.nl

Surf en Beach Strandhuisjes
Boulevard Zeezijde 9 - Opposite of
Boulevard 34 - 2225 BB Katwijk aan Zee
Tel. 06 – 22 80 97 24
www.surfenbeachstrandhuisjes.nl

Strandhuisjes De Watering
Strandvak 19 - 2225 AA Katwijk aan Zee
Tel. 06 - 55 13 47 50
www.de-watering.nl

Strandhuisjes Willy Noord
Strandvak 21 - 2225 WD Katwijk
Tel. 06 - 53 47 59 16
www.strandbungalowswillynoord.nl

Strandhuisjes Willy Zuid
Boulevard Zeezijde 51
2225 BB Katwijk
Tel. 071 - 401 37 33
www.strandhuisjeswillyzuid.nl

RESTAURANTS IN KATWIJK

De Beslagkom (Pancakes ≡ & Grill)
Prins Hendrikkade
Zwaaikom 3 2225 HX Katwijk
Tel. 071 - 407 80 07
www.debeslagkom.nl

In den Blauwen Bock ≡
Badstraat 9
2225 BL Katwijk
Tel. 071 - 401 52 73
www.blauwenbock.nl

De Bonte Kraai V
Princestraat 42
2225 GC Katwijk
Tel. 071 - 403 50 51
www.bontekraai.nl

Proeflokaal De Buuren ≡
Turfmarkt 2
2223 EH Katwijk
Tel. 071 - 403 01 19
www.proeflokaaldebuuren.nl

Bar 70 ≡
Boulevard 70
2225 AG Katwijk
Tel. 071 - 532 81 54
www.bar70.nl

Friends (Pancakes ≡, Pasta & Tapas)
Boulevard 68
2225 AG Katwijk
Tel. 071 - 401 00 09
www.friendskatwijk.nl

De Griek ≣
Voorstraat 42
2225 ER Katwijk
Tel. 071 - 401 08 81
www.degriekkatwijk.nl

Brasserie Havenkwartier ❚ ❚
Rogstraat 1
2224 TV Katwijk aan Zee
Tel. 071 - 529 49 22
www.brasserie-havenkwartier.nl

Jasmine Garden 🇨🇳
Hoornesplein 153
2221 BE Katwijk aan Zee
071 - 402 55 43
www.jasmine-garden.webnode.nl

Kam San 🇨🇳
Hoorneslaan 201-203
2221 CP Katwijk
Tel. 071 - 402 40 85
www.kamsan.nl

Pannekoekenboerderij (Pancakes≡)
Katwijk Wassenaarseweg 79
2223 LA Katwijk
Tel. 070 - 511 15 00
www.
pannenkoekenboerderijdehooiberg.
nl/index_katwijk.html

Sushi Katwijk 🇯🇵
Zwaaikom 6
2225 HX Katwijk
Tel. 088 - 247 00 00
www.sushikatwijk.nl

Krohr Katwijk 🇹🇭

Hans van der Hoevenstraat 176

2225 PX Katwijk

Tel. 071 - 301 64 59

www.thaikatwijk.nl

Eeterij Neefies 🇳🇱

E.A. Borgerstraat 28A

2225 AR Katwijk

Tel. 071 - 407 82 88

www.neefies.nl

Restaurant Noordzee / Bistro 🇳🇱🇮🇹

Pizzeria Boulevard 72

2225 AG Katwijk

Tel. 071 - 401 57 42

www.hotelnoordzee.nl

Het Panbos 🇳🇱🇮🇹

Wassenaarseweg 154

2223 LD Katwijk

Tel. 070 - 511 25 95

www.hetpanbos.nl

Restaurant Peking 🇨🇳

Wassenaarseweg 50a

2223 BL Katwijk

Tel. 071 - 402 97 06

www.pekingkatwijk.nl

Visrestaurant Schuitemaker 🇳🇱 (fish)

Voorstraat 9

2225 EJ Katwijk

Tel. 071 - 888 93 51

www.schuitemaker-vis.nl

Chinees Indisch

Restaurant Shanghai 🇨🇳

Jan van Brakelstraat 31

2224 RK Katwijk

Tel. 071 - 401 52 42

Argentijns Restaurant La Tapera 🇦🇷

Koningin Wilhelminastraat 16

2225 BA Katwijk

Tel. 071 - 407 54 42

www.latapera.nl

Grillbar Ruig (Grill)

Andreasplein 16

2225 GR Katwijk

Tel. 071 - 542 75 18

www.grillbarruig.nl

La Vida Loca 🇪🇸

Voorstraat 41

2225 EL Katwijk

Tel. 071 - 401 40 58

www.lavidalocakatwijk.nl

Het Wapen van Kattuk 🇳🇱🇮🇹

Sluisweg 2a

2225 XL Katwijk

Tel. 071 - 401 80 10

www.wapenvankattuk.nl

 Chinese cuisine   Dutch cuisine   Italian cuisine   Argentine cuisine

 Spanish cuisine   Greek cuisine   Japanese cuisine   French cuisine

 Thai cuisine   Vegetarian

BEACHRESTAURANTS IN KATWIJK

B.E.A.C.H (Mar-Oct)
Boulevard Zeezijde 3 /
Strandafgang 19
2225 BB Katwijk
Tel. 071 - 401 99 98
www.beachkatwijk.nl

Strandpaviljoen 't Centrum
(Feb-Oct)
BLVD Strandvak 11 -
Opposite of Boulevard 72
2225 AG Katwijk
Tel. 071 - 401 30 49
www.het-centrum.com

Kattukkerzandt
Boulevard Zeezijde 49
2225 BB Katwijk
Tel. 071 - 569 02 12
www.kattukkerzandt.nl

Strandhuys Katwijk
(open 365 days per year)
Boulevard Zeezijde 47
2225 BB Katwijk
Tel. 071 - 407 22 78
www.strandhuyskatwijk.nl

Beachhouse Key West (Mar-Sept)
Boulevard Zeezijde 11
2225 BB Katwijk
Tel. 06 - 22 19 64 69
www.beachhousekeywest.nl

KW106 (Mar-Oct)
Boulevard Zeezijde 41
Opposite of Boulevard 141
2225 DD Katwijk
Tel. 071 - 407 51 13
www.kw106.nl

Strandpaviljoen Paal 14
(open 365 days per year)
Boulevard Zeezijde 7
2225 AA Katwijk
Tel. 071 - 401 44 64
www.paal14.nl

Strandpaviljoen Sand C Bar
(Feb-Oct) Boulevard Zeezijde 43
2225 BB Katwijk
Tel. 071 - 401 48 18
www.sandcbar.nl

Sunset Beach (Feb-Oct)
Boulevard Zeezijde 35
2225 BB Katwijk
Tel. 071 - 401 23 14
www.sunsetbeachkatwijk.nl

Strandpaviljoen Surf en Beach
(Feb-Oct) Boulevard Zeezijde 9 /
Opposite of Boulevard 34
2225 BB Katwijk
Tel. 071 - 401 65 63
www.surfenbeach.nl

Het Strand (open 365 days per year)
Boulevard Zeezijde 23
2225 BB Katwijk
Tel. 071 - 401 20 48
www.het-strand.nl

Strandpaviljoen Het Wantveld
(Feb-Oct) Noordduinseweg 6
2221 BL Katwijk
Tel: 071 - 408 23 80
www.wantveldkatwijk.nl

Strandpaviljoen Willy Noord
(Mar-Oct) Strandweg 21
2225 WD Katwijk
Tel. 071 - 402 85 00
www.willynoord.nl

Strandpaviljoen Willy Zuid
(Mar-Sept) Boulevard 175
2225 HE Katwijk
Tel. 071 - 401 37 33
www.willyzuid.nl

Zee en Zon (Feb-Oct)
Boulevard Zeezijde 19
2225 BB Katwijk
Tel. 071 - 407 15 09
www.zeeenzon.nl

Strandpaviljoen Zilt
(open 365 days per year)
Boulevard Zeezijde 37
2225 BB Katwijk
Tel. 071 - 407 41 98
www.ziltstrand.nl

Beachclub Zomers (Feb-Oct)
Boulevard Zeezijde 21
2225 BB Katwijk
Tel. 071 - 401 28 10
www.zomersbeachclub.nl

1 - Laurentiuskerk, Kerkstraat 32, Rijnsburg

The Laurentius church is also called the Grote Kerk (Big Church) and was built in the year 1577 with materials from a former church from the Dorpsstraat (now Hoofdstraat) in Noordwijk. The church was built behind a Romanesque tower from the 12th century. This tower was the remainder of the abbey of Rijnsburg, which was founded in 1133 by Petronilla of Saxony and dowager Count Floris II of Holland.

After the church was put into use in 1578, it was expanded five times: in 1633, 1660, 1903, 1910 and 1923. In 1980 the church was closed for a year in connection with a major restoration. The entire roof was removed in order to be replaced. The Rijnsburg tower is, as with many other churches, the property of the bourgeois municipality. This dates back to the time of Napoleon, who, by a law in 1798, assigned almost all church towers to the municipality. In front of the church is the image of Floris V, Count of Holland and Zeeland and Lord of Friesland. This statue was unveiled in 2001 by Minister Korthals Altes. Floris V was probably buried in the abbey of Rijnsburg.

The Wilhelminaboom is located in the centre of the 'old' Rijnsburg. This was planted in 1898 in honor of the 18th birthday of Princess Wilhelmina. During the occupation years 1940-1945 the tree was the symbol of resistance against the occupier. The inscription and portrait were removed from the fence by order of the Germans. In the night of 30 to 31 of August 1941 (the birthday of Wilhelmina) the tree was festively decorated with orange flags and lanterns by a number of inhabitants. In the tense and overconfident atmosphere that arose in the village, many people spontaneously placed marigolds in the windows.

The occupier responded with a firm hand to this provocation and demanded that the decoration be removed immediately. This eventually led to riots in the village. On the 1st of September, a group of 30 random Rijnsburgs were arrested and imprisoned in the Oranjehotel penal prison in Scheveningen. The Germans tried to poison the tree a few days later, in which they did not succeed. The tree is still standing there today.

3

3 - Spinoza's house, Spinozalaan 29, Rijnsburg

The Dutch philosopher Baruch Spinoza lived in Rijnsburg from 1661 to 1663. He lived as a board member in a small room with surgeon Herman Hooman. He drew lenses for optical instruments and wrote his reflections with a goose pen.

Albert Einstein visited the Spinoza House on the 2nd of November 1920. Einstein later replied to the question whether he believed in God: "I believe in the God of Spinoza, who reveals himself in the legal harmony of the universe, and not in a God who interferes with the fate and actions of people." The Spinoza house has been used as a museum since 2012 and is open from Tuesday to Sunday from 1 pm to 5 pm.

For more information: www.spinozahuis.nl

De Vliet in
RIJNSBURG

WHERE TO STAY IN RIJNSBURG

Vakantiepark Koningshof
Elsgeesterweg 8
2231 NW Rijnsburg
Tel. 071 - 402 60 51

Zzz..

RESTAURANTS IN RIJNSBURG

Restaurant Aan de Vliet 🇫🇷
Vliet Noordzijde 73
2231 GR Rijnsburg
Tel. 071 - 889 12 99
www.restaurantaandevliet.nl

Brasserie de Burgt Burgemeester
(lunch / flammkuchen)
Koomansplein 1
2231 DA Rijnsburg
Tel. 071 - 408 77 74
www.brasseriedeburgt.nl

De Oude Keuken
(Wine restaurant)
Katwijkerweg 16
2231 SB Rijnsburg
Tel. 071 - 402 93 44 / 06 - 52 69 53 15
www.deoudekeuken.com

Chinees Restaurant Kwantung 🇨🇳
Tramstraat 3
2231 CJ Rijnsburg
Tel. 071 - 402 50 48

Restaurant Eetkafé Rijnsburg
🇳🇱 (Fingerfood)
Noordeinde 32
2231 LL Rijnsburg
Tel. 071 - 408 81 54
www.eetkafe.nl

Bar Bistro de Roos 🇳🇱🇫🇷
Valkenburgerweg 116
2231AP Rijnsburg
Tel. 071 - 402 06 83
www.bistroderoos.nl

De Taveerne
(holiday park Koningshof) 🇳🇱
Elsgeesterweg 8
2231 NW Rijnsburg
Tel. 071 - 402 60 51
www.koningshofholland.com

 Chinese cuisine   Dutch cuisine   🇫🇷 French cuisine

1

1 - Nederlands Hervormde Kerk,
Castellumplein 1, Valkenburg ZH

The Dutch Reformed church of Valkenburg is located at the Castellumplein. The name of the square refers to the castellum, a border fort on the Old Rhine, called Preatorium Aggripanae. This Roman settlement was located about 2,000 years ago where the village of Valkenburg now lies. Some of the excavations that have been done in the past can be seen in the Tower Museum.

In this museum you can also see a permanent exhibition about Valkenburg in the Second World War. During the May days of 1940, heavy fighting took place in and around Valkenburg. The museum is open on Saturday afternoon from 1 pm to 4 pm and further by appointment. The current church was only inaugurated in 1950, after the former church had largely been destroyed in this area during the Second World War. The church is part of the Protestant Church of the Netherlands.

2 - Former Town Hall, now Herberg Welgelegen,
't Boonrak 21, Valkenburg ZH

The former town hall of Valkenburg was built in 1895. At that time it was the home of a director of a pans factory on the Old Rhine.

From the thirties of the last century the building was inhabited by several families until it was put into use in 1968 for the wine trade. In 2014, the former town hall was renovated and since then it has the name Herberg Welgelegen. It is used as a wedding location, for retreat weekends, as a meeting location and you can spend the night there.

2

Z zz · ·
WHERE TO STAY IN VALKENBURG ZH

Herberg Welgelegen
Het Boonrak 21
2235 ED Valkenburg ZH
Tel. 06 - 51 79 94 95
www.herbergwelgelegen.nl

RESTAURANTS IN VALKENBURG ZH

Brasserie Buitenhuis ▬
J. Pellenbargweg 2
2235 SP Valkenburg ZH
Tel. 071 - 572 18 05
www.brasseriebuitenhuis.nl

Spijs & Wijn ▮▮
Voorschoterweg 23G
2235 SE Valkenburg ZH
Tel. 06 - 20 77 53 08
www.spijsenwijn.com

In het Wapen van Valkenburg ▬
Hoofdstraat 13
2235 CA Valkenburg ZH
Tel. 071 - 401 27 74

 Dutch cuisine ▮▮ French cuisine

Lisse
Heart of the Flower Region

Lisse, with the neighboring towns of De Engel and Halfweg and of course the Keukenhof, form the centre of the flower region. Lisse has about 23,000 inhabitants (2006). In 1998, Lisse celebrated her 800th anniversary. Possibly the village is much older. In a 1198 document, Lis is named for the first time, probably resulting from palisade or bulwark. The name of the square in the middle of Lisse with the name Vierkant (Square) refers to such a bulwark. In the Middle Ages, the people of Lisse (Dutch: Lissenaren) lived from agriculture, animal husbandry and turf cutting. Only later the flower bulb culture began to take shape in and around Lisse. More and more dunes were dug out for the purpose of flower bulb cultivation. The sandy soils, if at least fertilized, were ideal for flower bulb cultivation. This led to employment and great prosperity for the people of Lisse. The flower fields around Lisse, the Keukenhof and the annual

Flower Parade attract many tourists from home and abroad to Lisse and surrounding areas every year. Keukenhof is the most beautiful flower garden in the world and is visited annually by hundreds of thousands of people. In recent years, the number of visitors has even exceeded 1 million. The Keukenhof is part of the Keukenhof Estate, which also houses the Keukenhof Castle. In 1642 a court house was built, called 'Keukenhof' in the kitchen garden (Dutch: keukentuin) of Slot Teylingen. The yield of this dune area such as game, cattle, herbs and berries were destined for the kitchen of Slot Teylingen. In 1857 the park was redesigned by Zocher & zn landscaping architects who also designed the Amsterdam Vondelpark. The official opening of the flower exhibition took place in 1950. In 2003, the last castle lord of Keukenhof died. Since then, the Castle Keukenhof Foundation has the responsibility for the conservation and exploitation of the estate of more than 230 hectares of land and the 18 national monuments that stand on it. In the flower garden there are more than 7 million crocuses, daffodils, lilies, tulips, hyacinths and other flower bulbs. Guided tours are provided and you can make a trip through Keukenhof with a whistle boat between the bulb fields.

1 - 't Huys Dever, Heereweg 349-A, Lisse

't Huys Dever was built around 1375 by Reinier Dever or d'Ever. He was a member of a very old generation of Dutch nobility. The residential tower or Donjon, is a fortified house, many of which have stood in the coastal area. Dever is the only Donjon left. The back of the building was facing a swamp, the Lisser Poel. Because no danger threatened from that side, the back of the house is flat. The remaining walls are in the form of a horseshoe, solid masonry and almost 2 meters thick.

In 1848 the building collapsed partly due to poor foundation and neglect. In 1862 the roof collapsed. In the period from 1973 to 1978, 't Huys Dever was restored after which it was opened to the public. The construction is special because such Donjons have hardly been preserved in Holland due to, among other things, devastation (for example, prior to the Siege of Leiden), fire (Slot Teylingen) and radical renovations.

2 - H.H. Engelbewaarderskerk, Heereweg 457, Lisse

At the Heereweg in Lisse stands the striking, built in Neo-Byzantine style H.H. Engelbewaarderskerk. The church was built in 1930-1931 for the inhabitants of the small locality de Engel in Lisse. The church is owned by the parish Saint Willibrordus.

3 - Kasteel Keukenhof, Stationsweg 166, Lisse

Keukenhof castle was built in 1642 as a mansion by a former VOC commander in the Moluccas. For centuries, the castle has been inhabited by noble families. The last owner and resident was Jan Carel Elias count of Lynden (1912-2003). After his death, he left the castle, including the 230-hectare estate, behind to the Stichting Kasteel Keukenhof (Foundation Castle Keukenhof). This foundation aims to restore the castle and the estate including the 18 national monuments in the state in which they were beginning 1900. In 1642 a homestead was built with the name 'Keukenhof' in the kitchen garden of Slot Teylingen. The proceeds of this dune area such as game, cattle, herbs and berries were destined for the kitchen of Slot Teylingen, where among others Jacoba van Beieren lived. After a restoration of almost 2 years, Castle Keukenhof was reopened in 2012. The castle is an official wedding location and both the castle and the estate are used for (cultural) events. The carriage house next to the castle has also been restored. The gardens of the castle are open to the public.

On the estate is also the walled Frederiks Hof with the Swiss playhouse. The name Frederiks Hof comes from a boy of one of the noble families that have inhabited the castle. From the tradition it appears that Frederik was a gifted boy with a mental disorder. The playhouse was built for him around 1850 so that he could withdraw with a governess if the crowds were too much for him. The Frederiks Hof has also been completely restored.

4 - N.H. Kerk, Heereweg 250, Lisse

Around 1250 Count Willem II founded a chapel on "the green meadow of Lis". In 1460 the chapel was elevated by Pope Pius II to the parish church of Sint Agatha. It cannot be said with certainty whether this chapel stood on the same spot, but it is certain that the current church is built on remnants of the old parish church. The church is located on a high inner dune. During the 80-year war, around 1573/74, the church was destroyed. The church was later restored and became a reformed church. This reformed church remains the only officially recognized Christian church until the French era (1795), and it was not until 1826 that what was originally called the Reformed Church, was renamed as the Dutch Reformed Church.

The church underwent several restorations in the decades that follow. In 1915 the petroleum lighting was replaced by gas light which in 1922 again was replaced by electric light. In 1924 an extensive renovation took place. The northern side wing was added. The reason for this was to be able to cope with the resulting lack of space. In 2002-2003 there was again a major renovation. Space was then sacrificed for wider aisles and for a toilet group.

The church with the surrounding cemetery, the graveyard wall and the sexton's house form a beautiful whole. Both on the inside and on the outside of the church it is easy to see that the whole has arisen in different times. The church is now owned by the Protestant Church in the Netherlands (PKN; Protestantse Kerk in Nederland). The church board in Lisse ensures that non-members can also view the church inside. There are regular concerts but also openings where guided tours are given.

4

5+6

5 - Sint Agathakerk, Heereweg 273, Lisse

After the separation of church and state in 1796, the Roman Catholic inhabitants of Lisse wanted another church. They demanded back the village church on the Square. The beginning of a religious twist in Lisse. Only in 1842 could a church be built with financial support from King William I. However, it was not until 1902 that the construction of a new church actually started. In 1905 the boys' school was also built and in 1909 the Piusgesticht.

This 'Cathedral of the Flower Region' is dedicated to Agatha of Sicily (225-251). It is a 60-meter long three-aisled cross-church in Neo-Gothic style. The tower is 75 meters high, the highest in the Flower Region. In 1929 the upper part of the tower was replaced by the spire that now stands on the church. In the period 1993 - 2002 the church was radically restored. The Total restoration costs amounted to more than 3.5 million which was appealed to the inhabitants of Lisse. The church is owned by the parish Saint Willibrordus.

6 - Sint Agathaklooster, Heereweg 258, Lisse

The Sint Agatha monastery dates back to the 1900s. It was built on behalf of the RC parish Saint Agatha in Neo-Gothic style. The building was originally used by the Clarissen and the Sisters Fransciscanessen. The monastery has lost its original function over the years. It became a shelter for difficult to raise children. The building has been functioning as an office since 1984. The former chapel is used as a multifunctional space. This is used as a meeting room and concert hall.

7 - Station Lisse, Stationsweg 59, Lisse

Since 1842 the village of Lisse is already 'on the track'. However, it took until the end of the 19th century before the village would have its own railway station. At first it was not the intention that a station would come. The railway was intended to be a fast railway between Haarlem and Leiden without intermediate stations. During the construction there was a lot of resistance from the large landowners in the Flower Region. It was not until 1905 that Lisse got a full-fledged station. The high part of the building was the station residence. Because the station is so far from the village, it has never been able to meet the expectations and it was abolished in 1944. However, this did not mean a definite end. From the fifties until the end of the nineties, during the high season, daily trains stopped at the Lisse station for visitors to the Keukenhof. From 1994 the restaurant 'De Verloren Koffer' was located in the station building. Meanwhile, restaurant 'Het Tussenstation' has moved into the beautiful old station building.

7

WHERE TO STAY IN LISSE

Hotel

Hotel De Duif ★★★
Westerdreef 49
2161 EN Lisse
Tel. 0252 - 410 076
www.hoteldeduif.nl

Hotel De Nachtegaal ★★★★
Heereweg 10
2161 AG Lisse
Tel. 0252 - 433 030
www.nachtegaal.nl

Hotel De Engel
Heereweg 386
2161 DG Lisse
Tel. 0252 - 211 880
www.restaurant-de-engel.nl

Zzz..

Bed & Breakfast

B&B Madeleine
Heereweg 155
2161 BC Lisse
Tel. 06 - 15 62 17 60
www.bedandbreakfastmadeleine.nl

B&B 'Onder Ons'
Anne Frankstraat 8
2162 JP Lisse
Tel. 0252 - 420 043
www.bb-onderonslisse.nl

B&B De Vier Seizoenen
Heereweg 224
2161 BR Lisse
Tel. 0252 - 418 023
www.rdvs.nl

B&B De Zonnehoed
3e Poellaan76
2161 DN Lisse
Tel. 0252 - 214 376
www.dezonnehoed.nl

RESTAURANTS IN LISSE

Grand Café A-muze ▬
Heereweg 238
2161 BR Lisse
Tel. 0252 - 424 600
www.a-muze.com

Barista Café Lisse (lunch)
Blokhuis 20
2161 EW Lisse
Tel. 0252 - 751 843
www.baristacafelisse.nl

Brasserie de Buren ▬
Kanaalstraat 104
2161 JR Lisse
Tel. 0252 - 413 120
www.deburenlisse.nl

Cantina Sociale
Pane e Tulipani ▮▮
Heereweg 487
2161 DD Lisse
Tel. 0252 - 217 066
www.facebook.com/
PaneTulipani2012

Chefke's ▬ ▮▮
Grachtweg 15
2161 HL Lisse
Tel. 0252 - 410 389
www.chefkes.nl

China City ▮▮
Vivaldistraat 33
2162 AA Lisse
Tel. 0252 - 429 638
www.chinacity.wordpress.com

Chique en Simpel ▬ ▮▮
Heereweg 227
2161 BG Lisse
Tel. 0252 - 229 266
www.chiqueensimpel.nl

Restaurant De Engel ▬
Heereweg 386
2161 DG Lisse
Tel. 0252 - 211 880
www.restaurant-de-engel.nl

Restaurant Den Ouden Heere ▮▮
Heereweg 207a
2161 BE Lisse
Tel. 0252 - 418 660
www.denoudenheere.nl

Dragon Town ▮▮
Berkhoutlaan 5
2161 EL Lisse
Tel. 0252 - 414 018
www.dragontown.nl

Grand Café Cineac ▬ ▮▮
Floralisplein 69
2161 HX Lisse
Tel. 06 - 52 32 49 11
www.cineaclisse.nl

 Chinese cuisine  Dutch cuisine Italian cuisine

Spanish cuisine French cuisine

Cafetaria - Brasserie Family
(Grill & Pizza)
Blokhuis 24
2161 EW Lisse
Tel. 0252 - 421 282
www.lisse.family.nl

La Fontana 🇮🇹
Kanaalstraat 22
2161 JL Lisse
Tel. 0252 - 419 671
www.lafontana.nl

De Heerekamer 🇳🇱 🇮🇹
Heereweg 200/200a,
2161 BP Lisse
Tel. 0252 - 122 223
www.deheerekamer.nl

Brasserie Hemels (lunch)
Heereweg 232
2161 BR Lisse
Tel. 0252 - 347 521
www.brasseriehemels.nl

Restaurant Ibis (Grill)
Heereweg 230
2161 BR Lisse
Tel. 0252 - 418 486
www.restaurant-ibis.nl/#justeat

Itoshii 🇯🇵
Kanaalstraat 88b
2161 JP Lisse
Tel. 0252 - 410 864
www.itoshii.nl/sushi-lisse

Jardin (De Nachtegaal) 🇳🇱
Heereweg 10
2161 AG Lisse
Tel. 0252 - 433 030
www.nachtegaal.nl

Eetcafé Lef 🇳🇱 🇮🇹
Heereweg 234
2161 BR Lisse
Tel. 0252 - 411 665
www.eetcafelef.nl

Ristorante Il Mulino 🇮🇹
Heereweg 194
2161 BP Lisse
Tel. 06 - 28 18 11 48
www.ristoranteilmulino.nl

Trattoria da Marco 🇮🇹
Heereweg 207
2161 BE Lisse
Tel. 06 - 24 46 61 27
www.trattoriadamarco.nl

Mykonos

Kanaalstraat 90
2161 JP Lisse
Tel. 0252 - 420 760
www.mykonos-lisse.nl

Trattoria Panini 🇮🇹
Kanaalstraat 31
2161 JA Lisse
Tel. 0252 - 416 091
www.panini-lisse.nl

Ristorante Pizzeria Piccolo 🇮🇹

Heereweg 192,

2161 BP Lisse

Tel. 0252 - 414 496

www.restaurant-piccolo.nl

Dutch cuisine

Greek cuisine

Italian cuisine

Japanese cuisine

French cuisine

Qoffee & More (lunch)

Kanaalstraat 68

2161 JN Lisse

Tel. 06 - 29 11 91 60

www.facebook.com/

Qoffeeandmore

Restaurant Hofboerderij (lunch)

Keukenhof 1

2161 AN Lisse

Tel. 0252 - 750 690

www.kasteelkeukenhof.nl/nl/

ontdek-het-landgoed/

restaurant-hofboerderij

Het Tussenstation Lisse (lunch)

Stationsweg 59

2161 AM Lisse

Tel. 0252 - 422 202

www.hettussenstationlisse.nl

Vier Seizoenen 🇬🇷 🇮🇹

Heereweg 224

2161 BR Lisse

Tel. 0252 - 418 023

www.rdvs.nl

Vrouw Holle (Pancakes 🇳🇱)

Kanaalstraat 22

2161 JL Lisse

Tel. 0252 - 413 739

www.vrouwhollelisse.nl

Noordwijk

150 years seaside resort

The Zuid-Hollandse (South-Holland) municipality Noordwijk has more than 25,000 inhabitants. The year 2016 was in the mark of Noordwijk, 150 years seaside resort. Traditionally, Noordwijk was a fishing village. The village has two village centres; Noordwijk aan Zee and Noordwijk-Binnen. The old core of Noordwijk-Binnen radiates the tranquility of earlier centuries. Walking in the vicinity of the Voorstraat and the Lindenplein, you will experience times gone by. Here you will find ancient small laborers houses and beautiful monumental villas, old village pumps, a music chapel and the two major churches of Noordwijk that mark the ancient village centre from afar.

South of Noordwijk-Binnen is another small locality called De Klei. Until the 19th century, fishing was especially important for the village. After that, tourism for the inhabitants of Noordwijk has become the main source of income. Every year more than 1 million spend the night in Noordwijk. Along the boulevard of Noordwijk there are many hotels and restaurants and there is a wide range of nightlife. The shopping streets in Noordwijk aan Zee have been open on Sundays for years and Noordwijk belongs to one of the richest parts of the Netherlands. On the list of 50 richest neighbourhoods in the Netherlands, Noordwijk stands at number 12. Especially in the villa district the Zuidduinen you will find beautiful villas in the dune landscape. The Noordwijks dialect, which strongly resembles Katwijks and Schevenings, is still spoken by a small proportion of the native people.

Probably around 2000 years before Christ, people already lived in the place we call Noordwijk-Binnen. Around the year 1200, Noordwijk aan Zee was inhabited for the first time, presumably by fishermen. Jeroen van Noordwijk, a Scottish Benedictine monk, did missionary work and built a chapel in Noordwijk around 850. A few years later, he was captured by Northmen and beheaded after. Around 980, a Romanesque chapel was built in honor of him, which was replaced in 1303 by a stone church, which was later replaced by Saint Jeroen Church (Sint Jeroenskerk). In 889, the Count of West Frisia received a letter from the King of Lorraine, in which it was stated that he would receive Northgo as collateral (the old name of Noordwijk). Northgo meant 'Go (or gouw) to the north', which stood for something like 'residence north of the Rhine'. The bishop of Utrecht declared Noordwijk to place of pilgrimage in 1429. The suspected skull of Saint Jeroen was the main relic. Due to a large fire in Noordwijk-Binnen in the year 1450 the church was completely destroyed. The Reformation in the 16th century made an end to Noordwijk as a place of pilgrimage.

Enough history; time to explore Noordwijk. Enjoy relaxing on the beach, enjoy going out, enjoy culinary delights, stay at a seaside campsite at the coast or in a luxurious 5-star hotel, all is possible in Noordwijk. It's not without a reason that already for 150 years Noordwijk has been the most beautiful seaside resort in the Netherlands!

SightsinNoordwijk

1

1 - **Dorpspomp,** Voorstraat, Noordwijk

In the heart of Noordwijk-Binnen there are three old village pumps. These pumps originate from the second half of the 18th century. In addition to the water supply, the pumps also had an important social function. They formed a meeting place for the population to exchange the latest village news.

2 - **Lindenhof,** Lindenplein 1, Noordwijk

The Lindenhof is a 17th century country house and was the first Latin school in Noordwijk. Later it was used as a notary's house and as an outdoor clinic of the Academic Hospital. It is also the birthplace of writer and poet Henriette Roland Holst-van der Schalk (1869-1952). A bust of her was placed in front of her birth house in 1969.

2

3

3 - Town Hall, Voorstraat 42, Noordwijk
The town hall dates from the year 1887. It is built in neoclassical style.

4

4 - Hoogewegse Molen, Leidsevaart, Noordwijk
This mill located between Voorhout and Noordwijk from 1652 was largely renovated in 1711 and restored in 1995. The mill takes care of the drainage of the Hoogewegpolder. The mill is 9 meters high and the flight of the blades is 17,3 meters. Since 1961 the Rijnlandse Molenstichting (Mill Foundation) owns the mill.

HoogewegseMolen
NOORDWIJK

5

5 - Oude Jeroenskerk, Voorstraat 44, Noordwijk

The Oude Jeroenskerk is located in the centre of Noordwijk-Binnen. Formerly also known as the Grote (Big) or St. Jeroenskerk. The church is named after the martyr Jeroen who was beheaded in 856 because he did not want to lose his faith. The church is owned by the Protestant Municipality in Noordwijk.

The tower of the church is 40 meters high. Legend tells us that Jeroen's skull has been buried in the church. In 1983, a young man's skull was unearthed in the choir that might have been from Jeroen.

On the site of the Old Jeroen, a wooden church stood between 856 and 988 and presumably thereafter a church made of tuff bricks. In 1450 there was a big fire in the church. In 1573 the church passed from being a Catholic church to a Reformed one. Since 1798 the tower has been owned by the Municipality of Noordwijk. In 1860 a house of preservation was built on the Voorstraat in Noordwijk. Until then, convicts were imprisoned in one of the two cells located in the tower. From April to October the tower can be visited on Saturdays from noon to 4 pm.

6 - Sint Jeroenskerk, Van Limburg Stirumstraat 24, Noordwijk

The Sint Jeroenskerk is named after Sint Jeroen who dedicated a church to Sint Maarten in 851 in Noordwijk. In 856 he was killed and decapitated by Vikings. A church was built at the place where his body was found. During excavation work at the church around 1300 a skull was found which was assumed to belong to Sint Jeroen. The skull was kept in the church and in 1429 Noordwijk was proclaimed pilgrimage place for Saint Jeroen.

The old Sint Jeroenskerk passed from the Catholics to the Protestants during the Reformation. That is why a new Catholic church was built in 1834. The church is currently used by the parish Sint Jeroen and Maria ter Zee which since 2011 is part of the Sint Maartensparochie (Saint Martin Parish).

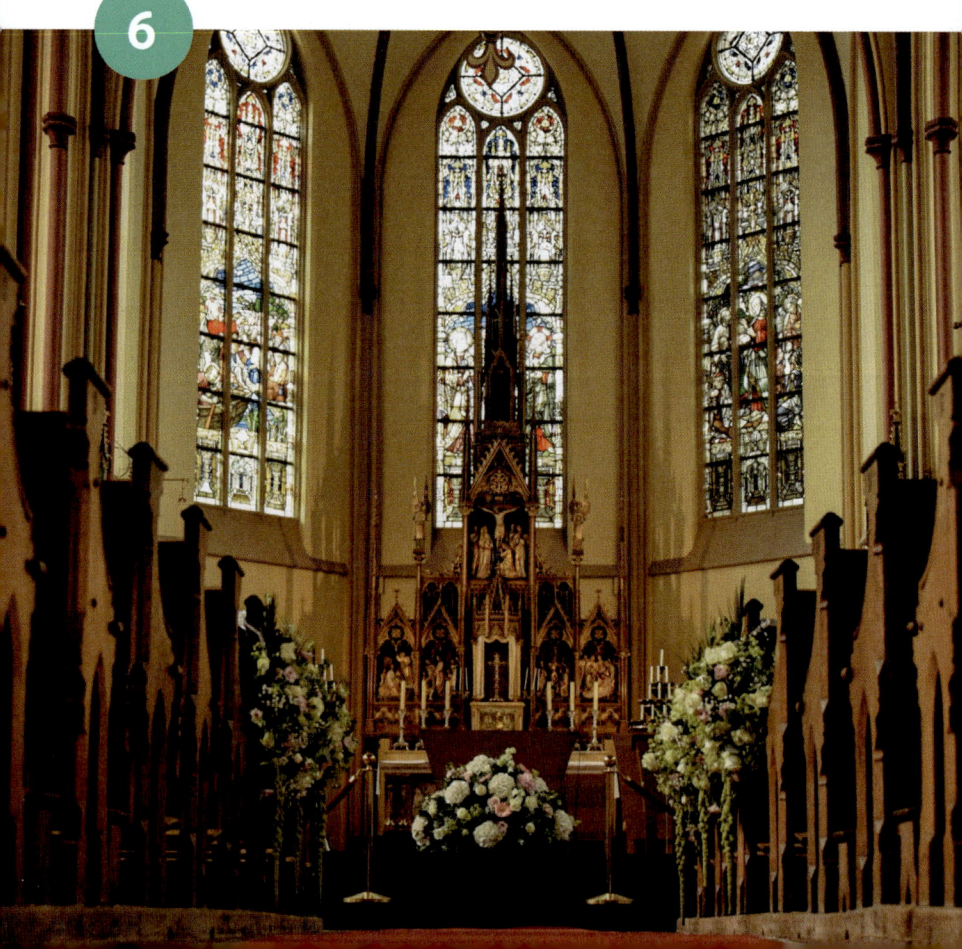

6

7
7 - Lighthouse Noordwijk aan Zee,
Koningin Wilhelmina boulevard 34, Noordwijk

Since 1444, after sunset, a fire was ignited on the beaches of Noordwijk to point fishermen to the coast. Only when there were fishermen at sea, the light was ignited. A wooden scaffolding was built in the 19th century and in 1854 it was replaced by a stone tower. In 1913 it was broken down. The lighthouse that now stands there is made of brick and reinforced concrete and was built in 1921 as a reconnaissance light for shipping. To prevent water leakage, a white plaster layer was later applied. The last lighthouse keeper, Dick van Dee, was in function from 1954-1986. Since then the tower has been unmanned. Since 1980, the lighthouse has only been opened on special occasions such as on Heritage Days. The tower has been restored in 2004.

By the beach,
near the sea,
whata**wonderful**
place to be

WHERE TO STAY
IN NOORDWIJK

Hotel

Hotel Aan Zee ★
Parallel Boulevard 206
2202 HT Noordwijk
Tel. 071 - 361 29 19
www.hotelaanzee.nl

Hotel de Admiraal ★★★
Quarles van Uffordstraat 81
2202 ND Noordwijk
Tel. 071 - 361 24 60
www.hoteladmiraal.nl

Alexander Hotel ★★★★
Oude Zeeweg 63
2202 CJ Noordwijk
Tel. 071 - 361 89 00
www.alexanderhotel.nl

Hotel Astoria ★★★
Emmaweg 13
2202 CP Noordwijk
Tel. 071 - 361 00 14
www.hotelastoria.nl

Fletcher Badhotel Noordwijk ★★★
Julianastraat 32
2202 KD Noordwijk aan Zee
Tel. 071 -362 03 40
www.badhotelnoordwijk.nl

De Baak Seaside ★★★
Kon. Astrid Boulevard 23
2202 BJ Noordwijk
Tel. 071 - 369 04 84
www.debaakseaside.nl

Beach Hotel Noordwijk ★★★★
Kon. Wilhelmina Boulevard 31
2202 GW Noordwijk
Tel. 071 - 367 68 77
www.beachhotelnoordwijk.com

Flying Pig Beach Hostel
Parallel Boulevard 208
2202 HT Noordwijk
Tel. 071 - 362 25 33
www.flyingpig.nl/beach

Golden Tulip Noordwijk ★★★★
Koningin Wilhelmina Boulevard 8
2202 GS Noordwijk
Tel. 071 - 361 92 05
www.goldentulipnoordwijkbeach.nl

Hotel Golfzicht ★★★
Golfweg 15
2202 JG Noordwijk
Tel. 071 - 361 92 08
www.golfzicht.nl

Heeren van Noortwyck ★★★
Quarles van Uffordstraat 103
2202 NE Noordwijk
Tel. 071 - 361 27 23
www.heerenvannoortwyck.nl

Zzz..

Hightop Hotel ★★★
Prins Hendrikweg 19
2202 EC Noordwijk aan Zee
Tel. 071 - 361 24 89
www.hightophotel.nl

Hogerhuys ★★★★
Emmaweg 25
2202 CP Noordwijk
Tel. 071 - 361 73 00
www.hogerhuys.nl

Grand Hotel Huis ter Duin ★★★★★
Koningin Astrid Boulevard 5
2202 BK Noordwijk aan Zee
Tel. 071 - 361 92 20
www.huisterduin.com

Zorghotel de Kim (care hotel)
Rembrandtweg 2
2202 AX Noordwijk
Tel. 071 - 364 07 30
www.zorghoteldekim.nl

Hotel de Koningshof ★★★
Golfbaan 66
2202 TE Noordwijk
Tel. 071 - 361 32 71
www.hoteldekoningshof.nl

Hotel van Oranje ★★★★★
Koningin Wilhelmina Boulevard 20
2202 GV Noordwijk
Tel. 071 - 367 68 69
www.hotelvanoranje.com

De Ossewa ★★★
Duinweg 7
2202 RA Noordwijk
Tel. 071 - 361 21 39
www.osewa.nl

Radisson Blu Palace Hotel ★★★★
Pickeplein 8
2202 CL Noordwijk
Tel. 071 - 365 30 00
www.radissonblu.com/nl/
palacehotel-noordwijk

Prominent Inn Hotel ★★★★
Koningin Wilhelmina Boulevard 4
2202 GR Noordwijk
Tel. 071 - 361 22 53
www.prominentinn.nl

Hotel Royal ★★★
Voorstraat 76
2201 HZ Noordwijk
Tel. 071 - 364 65 12
www.hotelroyal.nl

Stayokay Noordwijk ★★
Langevelderlaan 45 - Noordwijk
Tel. 0252 - 372 920
www.stayokay.com/en/hostel/
noordwijk

Vesper Hotel ★★★★
Koningin Astrid Boulevard 46
2202 BE Noordwijk
Tel. 071 - 800 99 88
www.vesperhotel.com

Hotel

Villa de Duinen ★★★
Oude Zeeweg 74
2202 CE Noordwijk
Tel. 071 - 364 89 32
www.villadeduinen.nl

Fletcher Hotel Restaurant
De Witte Raaf ★★★★
Duinweg 117-119
2204 AT Noordwijk
Tel. 0347 - 750 449
www.fletcherhoteldewitteraaf.nl

Hotel Zonne ★★★
Rembrandtweg 17
2202 AT Noordwijk
Tel. 071 - 361 96 00
www.hotelzonne.nl

Zorn Hotel Duinlust ★★★
Koepelweg 1
2202 AJ Noordwijk aan Zee
Tel. 071 - 361 29 16
www.hotelzorn.nl

Bed & Breakfast

Aan Zee en Duin
Kraaierslaan 32
2204 AP Noordwijk
Tel. 0252 - 344 616

Klein Boerenburg
Langevelderlaan 6a
2204 BD Noordwijk
Tel. 06 - 55 72 84 69

Charme aan Zee
Langevelderlaan 15
2204 BC Noordwijk
Tel. 06 - 52 52 83 48

Georgettes Beach Guesthouse
Beethovenweg 8
2202 AH Noordwijk
Tel. 06 - 19 43 27 39
www.facebook.com/
GeorgettesGuesthouse

L'Hirondelle
Daniel Noteboomstraat 30
2202 RL NOORDWIJK
Tel. 06 - 25 20 60 12

Huisje Kroon
Duindamseweg 12F (12-6)
2204 AS Noordwijk
Tel. 06 - 30 77 74 16

Pension 't Hofje
Golfbaan 43 2202
TD Noordwijk
Tel. 071 - 361 33 43

Liquenda B&B
Quarles van Uffordstraat 32
2202 NH Noordwijk
Tel. 06 - 12 32 05 62

Maria's B&B
Alk 53
2201 XL Noordwijk
Tel. 071 - 362 21 41

Noordwijk Binnen B&B
Wilhelminastraat 25,
2201 KA Noordwijk
Tel. 071 - 341 13 22

Pirombo B&B
Oude Zeeweg 22
2201 TB Noordwijk
Tel. 071 - 361 31 18
www.pirombo-noordwijk.nl

Stranghusje
Quarles van Uffordstraat 13
2202 NB Noordwijk
Tel. 071 - 364 76 24

Violet's B&B
Beatrixtraat 24
2202 NR Noordwijk
Tel. 06 - 20 38 60 77
www.bedandbreakfast-noordwijk.com

WIT51
Van Panhuysstraat 51
2203 JP Noordwijk
Tel. 071 - 362 00 60
www.wit51.nl

Zeebries
Daniël Noteboomstraat 36
2202 RL Noordwijk
Tel. 06 - 53 75 65 53

De Zonnepit
Duizendblad 56 2201 SR Noordwijk
Tel. 071 - 362 91 00
www.dezonnepit.nl

Campings / Bungalows

Camping de Carlton
Kraaierslaan 13
2204 AN Noordwijk
Tel. 0252 - 372 783
www.campingdecarlton.nl

Camping De Duinpan
Duindamseweg 6
2204 AS Noordwijk
Tel. 0252 - 371 726
www.campingdeduinpan.com

Camping Le Parage
Langevelderlaan 43
2204 BC Noordwijk
Tel. 0252 - 375 671
www.sollasi.nl/le-parage

Caravanpark The Relaxing Crow
Kraaierslaan 27
2204 AN Noordwijk
Tel. 0252 - 373 467
www.the-relaxing-crow.jouwweb.nl

Camping De Ruigenhoek
Vogelaardreef 31
2204 AA Noordwijk
Tel. 0252 - 375 002
www.goedkamp.nl

Camping de Wulp
Kraaierslaan 25 2204
AN Noordwijk
Tel. 0252 - 372 826
www.dewulp.com

Vakantiepark Duinrust
Randweg 6
2204 AL Noordwijk
Tel. 0252 - 372 425
www.vakantieparkduinrust.com

Bungalowpark De Gouden Spar
Duinweg 102
2204 AW Noordwijk
Tel. 0252 - 372 771
www.goudenspar.nl

Bungalowpark 't Lappennest
Duinweg 90
2204 AW Noordwijk
Tel. 0252 - 376 388
www.lappennest.nl

Recreatiepark Noordwijkse Duinen
Kapelleboslaan 41
2204 AJ Noordwijk
www.noordwijkseduinen.nl

Bungalowpark Puik en Duin
Duinweg 80
2204 AW Noordwijk
Tel. 0252 - 344 738
www.puikenduin.nl

Parc du Soleil
Kraaierslaan 7
2204 AN Noordwijk
Tel. 088 - 500 24 52
www.parcdusoleil.nl

Bungalowparck Tulp en Zee

Randweg / Tulp & Zee 1

2204 CW Noordwijk

Tel. 0252 - 372 515

www.tulpenzee.nl

Buitenplaats Witte Raaf aan Zee

/ Ravenhof / Bullewei /

Duinpark de Witte Raaf

Duindamseweg 7

2204 AR Noordwijk

Tel. 0252 - 361 100

www.noordwijkvakanties.nl

Beach Houses

Take2 Beach & Bungalows

Koningin Astrid Boulevard 84

2202 BD Noordwijk

Tel. 071 - 364 87 90

www.take2noordwijk.nl/nl/slapen/

slapen-op-het-strand

RESTAURANTS IN NOORDWIJK

Eeterij de Beleving 🇳🇱
Kraaierslaan 7
2204 AN Noordwijk
Tel. 0252 - 370 410
www.eeterijdebeleving.nl

Bij Raggers 🇳🇱
Wilhelminaboulevard 16A
2202 GT Noordwijk
Tel. 071 - 361 48 75
www.bijraggers.nl

De Blauwe Gans 🇳🇱
Koningin Wilhelmina Boulevard 4
2202 GR Noordwijk
Tel. 071 - 361 22 53
www.prominentinn.nl/restaurant

De Botter 🇳🇱 (fish)
Koningin Wilhelmina Boulevard
16B-C 2202 GT Noordwijk
Tel. 071 - 361 15 20
www.restaurantdebotter.nl

Proeflokaal Bregje 🇳🇱
Herenweg 227 - 2201 AG Noordwijk
Tel 071 - 301 60 59
www.proeflokaalbregje.nl

Brasserie & Terrace Circles / Dunes Lounge & Bar 🇫🇷
Pickeplein 8
2202 CL Noordwijk
Tel. 071 - 365 30 00
www.radissonblu.com/en/
palacehotel-noordwijk/restaurants

Chicoleo Mexican & Steakhouse 🇲🇽
Koningin Wilhelmina Boulevard 7b
2202 GR Noordwijk
Tel. 071 - 361 21 21
www.chicoleo-noordwijk.nl

Copper 🇳🇱🇫🇷
Grent 1 2202 EJ Noordwijk
Tel. 071 - 368 18 02
www.coppernoordwijk.nl

La Cubanita 🇪🇸
Koningin Wilhelmina Boulevard 12a
2202 GT Noordwijk
Tel. 071 - 361 90 70
www.lacubanita.nl/tapas-noordwijk

De Duinrand 🇳🇱
Duindamseweg 17
2204 AR Noordwijk
Tel. 0252 - 372 370
www.restaurantdeduinrand.nl

Dutch! 🇳🇱
Koningin Wilhelmina boulevard 31
2202 GW Noordwijk
Tel. 071 - 367 68 54
www.hotelvanoranje.nl/restaurant-
noordwijk-aan-zee/restaurant-dutch

Dylans 🇳🇱🇫🇷
Oude Zeeweg 63
2202 CJ Noordwijk
Tel. 071 - 364 07 77
www.dylansnoordwijk.nl

Restaurant Emma ══
Emmaweg 25 2202 CP Noordwijk
Tel. 071 - 361 73 00
www.hogerhuys.nl/nl/emma-
dinner-drinks

't Elfde Gebod ══
Koningin Wilhelmina Boulevard 28
2202 GW Noordwijk
Tel. 071 - 367 68 35
www.hotelvanoranje.nl/restaurant-
noordwijk-aan-zee/grand-cafe-t-
elfde-gebod

La Galleria ▌▌
Koningin Wilhelmina Boulevard 18
2202 GT Noordwijk
Tel. 071 - 361 71 96
www.lagalleria.nl/restaurants/
boulevard-noordwijk

De Gouden Muur ▨
Koningin Wilhelmina Boulevard 14
2202 GT Noordwijk
Tel. 071 - 361 79 49
www.de-gouden-muur.nl

Hans en Grietje (Pancakes ══)
Parallel Boulevard 14
2202 HP Noordwijk
Tel. 071 - 361 08 74
www.pannenkoekenhuisje.nl

The Harbourlights ══ ⊞
Koningin Wilhelmina Boulevard 9
2202 GT Noordwijk
Tel. 071 - 361 77 05
www.harbourlights.nl

Steakhouse De Harmonie (Grill)
Koningin Wilhelmina Boulevard 20
2202 GV Noordwijk
Tel. 071 - 367 68 69
www.hotelvanoranje.nl/culinair/
steakhouse-de-harmonie

Heeren van Noortwijck ══
Quarles van Uffordstraat 103
2202 NE Noordwijk
Tel. 071 - 361 27 23
www.heerenvannoortwyck.nl

Hiromina ◉
Koningin Wilhelmina Boulevard 9 a/b
2202 GT Noordwijk
Tel. 071 - 361 04 46
www.hiromina.nl

Hof van Holland ══ ▌▌
Voorstraat 79
2201 HP Noordwijk
Tel. 071 - 361 22 55
www.hofvanhollandnoordwijk.nl

Hoogies ══
(open in summertime only)
Langevelderslag 28-30
2204 AH Noordwijk
www.bijhoogies.nl

Iets Anders 🇫🇷
Pickeplein 4 - 2202 CK Noordwijk
Tel. 071 - 361 11 36
www.restaurant-ietsanders.nl

Kabbour Tapas y Gamba's 🇪🇸
De Grent 12 - 2202 EL Noordwijk
Tel. 071 - 361 41 30
www.kabbour.nl

De Klucht 🇳🇱
Abraham van Royenstraat 108
2202 EP Noordwijk
Tel. 071 - 361 91 72
www.dekluchtnoordwijk.nl

Ko Sing 🇮🇳 🇨🇳
Kerkstraat 79 - 2201 KL Noordwijk
Tel. 071 - 361 33 08
www.kosing.nl

De Lamme Goedzak 🇳🇱
Parallel Boulevard 18
2202 HP Noordwijk
Tel. 071 - 361 20 83
www.lammegoedzak.nl

Langs Berg en Dal
(Pancakes 🇳🇱 & more)
Langevelderlaan 22
2204 BD Noordwijk
Tel. 0252 - 372 474
www.langsbergendal.nl

Latour 🇫🇷 **1 Michelin Star**
Koningin Astrid Boulevard 5
2202 BK Noordwijk
Tel. 071 - 365 12 39
www.restaurantlatour.nl

Eetcafe Restaurant 't Lieverdje 🇳🇱
Kerkstraat 48
2201 KN Noordwijk
Tel. 071 - 362 27 16
www.lieverdjenoordwijk.com

Malegijs 🇳🇱 (fish)
Koningin Wilhelminaboulevard 13
2202 GT Noordwijk
Tel. 071 - 361 09 60
www.malegijs.nl

Mimmo 🇮🇹
Koningin Wilhelmina
Boulevard 16/2202
2202 GT Noordwijk
Tel. 071 - 362 44 77
www.mimmo.nl

Mizumi 🇯🇵
Kerkstraat 73
2201 KL Noordwijk
Tel. 071 - 767 60 08
www.facebook.com/
MizumiNoordwijk

Brasserie Noordzee 🇳🇱
Koningin Wilhelmina Boulevard 8
2202 GS Noordwijk
Tel. 071 - 361 92 05
www.brasserienoordzee.nl

Onder de Linde 🇳🇱 🇫🇷
Voorstraat 133
2201 HS Noordwijk
Tel. 071 - 362 31 97
www.onderdelinde.com

Open Doors (Grill)
De Grent 34
2202 EL Noordwijk
Tel. 071 - 361 48 80
After 22.00 hrs Late Night Kitchen
www.open-doors.nl

Oriento
Koningin Wilhelmina Boulevard 20
2202 GV Noordwijk
Tel. 071 - 367 68 52
www.hotelvanoranje.nl/culinair/
oriento-asian-inspired-cuisine

't Pannekoekenhuisje (Pancakes 🇳🇱)
Koningin Wilhelmina Boulevard
15a-15b 2202 Noordwijk
Tel. 071 - 361 68 50
www.hetpannekoekenhuisje.nl

Pinocchio 🇮🇹
Parallel Boulevard 2
2202 HP Noordwijk
Tel. 071 - 361 82 33
www.pizzeriapinocchio.nl

Pitch 🇳🇱
Van Berckelweg 38
2203 LB Noordwijk
Tel. 071 - 362 91 88
www.pitchnoordwijk.nl

Café Rosser 🇳🇱
De Grent 10
2202 EL Noordwijk
Tel. 06 - 22 58 87 11
www.caferosser.nl

Hotel Royal 🇳🇱 🇫🇷
Voorstraat 76
2201 HZ Noordwijk
Tel. 071 - 364 65 12
www.royaletenendrinken.nl

Schitzelparadijs (Schnitzels!)
Koningin Wilhelmina Boulevard 7a
2202 GR Noordwijk
Tel. 071 - 361 95 60
www.schnitzelparadijs-noordwijk.nl

Sunand Anglo-Indian Restaurant 🇮🇳
Bomstraat 46
2202 GH Noordwijk
Tel. 071 - 361 80 99
www.sunand.nl

Taj Mahal 🇮🇳
Parallel Boulevard 2
2202 HP Noordwijk
Tel. 071 - 362 29 90
www.tajmahal-noordwijk.nl

Brasserie la Terrasse 🇫🇷

Koningin Astrid Boulevard 5

2202 BK Noordwijk

Tel. 071 - 361 92 20

www.restaurantlaterrasse.nl

Proeflokaal Thomas 🇳🇱

Heilige Geestweg 2

2201 JS Noordwijk

Tel. 06 - 20 66 32 34

www.proeflokaalthomas.nl

Tong AH

De Grent 36

2202 EL Noordwijk

Tel. 071 - 361 29 82

www.tongah-noordwijk.nl

Ristorante Fratelli 🇮🇹

Koningin Wilhelmina Boulevard 5

2202 GR Noordwijk

Tel. 071 - 361 65 55

www.fratelli.nl

Vesper Hotel

Koningin Astrid Boulevard 46

2202 BE Noordwijk

Tel. 071 - 800 99 88

www.vesperhotel.com

Villa de Duinen 🇳🇱 🇫🇷

Oude Zeeweg 74

2202 CE Noordwijk

Tel. 071 - 364 89 32

www.villadeduinen.nl

Café De Wels 🇳🇱

Abraham van Royenstraat 8

2202 EN Noordwijk

Tel. 071 - 361 27 35

www.cafedewels.nl

Wish You Were Hier

Koningin Wilhelmina Boulevard 15

2202 GT Noordwijk

Tel. 071 - 889 99 37

www.wywh.world

Fletcher Hotel Restaurant 🇳🇱
De Witte Raaf

Duinweg 117

2204 AT Noordwijk

Tel. 0252 - 242 900

www.fletcherhoteldewitteraaf.nl

Yan 🇹🇭

Albert Verweystraat 50

2202 NP Noordwijk

Tel. 071 - 364 88 88

www.yannoordwijk.nl

Zonneweelde 🇳🇱

Duindamseweg 8

2204 AS Noordwijk

Tel. 0252 - 372 524

www.restaurantzonneweelde.nl

	Chinese cuisine		Dutch cuisine		Italian cuisine
	Spanish cuisine		Japanese cuisine		Indian cuisine
	English cuisine		French cuisine		Thai cuisine

BEACHRESTAURANTS IN NOORDWIJK

Alexander Beach Club
(open 365 days per year)
Koningin Wilhelmina Boulevard
Afrit (exit) 10
Tel. 071 - 362 04 89
www.alexanderbeach.nl

Branding Beachclub
(Mar-Sep) / Winter Lodge (Oct- Feb)
Koningin Astridboulevard 105
Afrit (exit) 4, Noordwijk
Tel. 071 - 511 30 30
www.brandingbeach.nl -
www.winterlodge.nl

Breakers Beach House
(open 365 days per year)
Koningin Astrid Boulevard 5
2202 BK Noordwijk
Tel. 071 - 365 14 81
www.breakersbeachhouse.nl

Strandpaviljoen Blu Beach
(open 365 days per year)
Koningin Wilhelmina Boulevard 104
2202 GW Noordwijk
Tel. 071 - 362 04 90
www.blubeach.nl

Beachclub Bries (Mar-Sept)
Koningin Astrid Boulevard
102 Afrit (exit) 2,
2202 BD Noordwijk
Tel. 071 - 361 78 91
www.briesnoordwijk.nl

B.E.A.C.H. Noordwijk (Mar-Sept)
Koningin Wilhelminaboulevard
Afrit (exit) 19
2202 GT Noordwijk
Tel. 071 - 362 47 25
www.deklink.info

Strandpaviljoen De Koele Costa
(Mar-Oct) Zeereep 21
2202 Noordwijk
Tel. 06 - 43 74 79 35
www.dekoelecosta.nl

Strandrestaurant Nederzandt
(open 365 days per year)
Langevelderslag 36-56
2204 AH Noordwijk
Tel. 0252 - 372 430
www.nederzandt.nl

Beachclub O (open 365 days per year)
Koningin Wilhelmina Boulevard 106
2202 GW Noordwijk
Tel. 071 - 367 68 94
www.beachclubo.nl

Take2 Beach Strandpaviljoen
(Feb-Oct)
Koningin Astrid Boulevard 101
2202 BD Noordwijk
Tel. 071 - 364 87 90
www.take2noordwijk.nl

Tulum Tulum
Zeereep 104
2202 Noordwijk
Tel. 071 - 511 21 21
www.tulumtulum.nl

Strandpaviljoen Van Roon
(Mar-Sept) Koningin Wilhelmina
Boulevard 105 Afrit (exit) 14
2202 GW Noordwijk
Tel. 071 - 361 33 05
www.strandjvanroon.nl

Strandclub Witsand (Mar-Sept)
Zeereep 103 2202 NW Noordwijk
Tel. 071 - 511 20 20
www.strandclubwitsand.nl

Strandpaviljoen de Zeemeeuw
(open 365 days per year)
Koningin Wilhelmina Boulevard 108
Afrit (exit) 18 2202 GW Noordwijk
Tel. 071 - 362 52 95
www.zeemeeuw.com

Strandpaviljoen De Zeespiegel
(Apr-Sept) Duindamseslag 1
Afrit (exit) 24 2204 AM Noordwijk
Tel. 0252 - 376 790
www.strandpaviljoendezeespiegel.nl

Zon & Zeebad
(open 365 days per year)
Koningin Astrid Boulevard 107
2202 BD Noordwijk
Tel. 071 - 361 33 35
www.zonenzeebad.nl

Strandpaviljoen Het Zuiderbad
(open 365 days per year)
Koningin Astridboulevard 104
2202 BD Noordwijk
Tel. 071 - 362 05 51
www.zuiderbad.nl

Het Stalhuis - Klein Leeuwenhorst

Noordwijkerhout
Easy-going and hospitable

With the largest area of colorful flower bulb fields of the region, Noordwijkerhout calls itself 'Heart of the Bulb Region'. The village has more than 16,000 inhabitants.

Like Hillegom and Lisse, Noordwijkerhout has also been formed on a beach shore. Strandwallen (Beach Walls) are remnants of the old dunes that formed after the ice age. In the area that is now called Langeveld, the first inhabitants settled. During the Roman era there lived a Germanic tribe; the Caninefaaten. This name is honored by one of the four carnival associations known to the village, the Kaninefaaten. Before the Middle

Ages there was a road from Noordwijk (then Northgo) to 'den Grooten Hout', a forest east of Noordwijk. At a hunting lodge that was standing there at that time, the village of Noortiger-hout originated. The name of the county of Holland, which descends from Holtland (Houtland, in English: Woodland), indicates that the area must have been very woody. In the municipal archives, documents were found from 1231 which show that the legacy of Count Gerolf was divided between his two sons. One of them got Nortich (Northgo) and the other Nortich in den Houte in other words Noordwijkerhout.

For centuries, the inhabitants of Noordwijkhout lived largely from arable farming and livestock farming. They experienced a lot of trouble from large numbers of dune rabbits who ate the crops. Alternative sources of entry were sought in shellfish fishing, by poaching or by beachcombers. In the seventeenth century a lot of flax was cultivated and processed in Noordwijkerhout. Rich notables from neighboring cities built outbuildings in the 17th and 18th centuries, which also caused additional income and employment. In the second half of the 19th century began the digging out of the old beach walls. The sand was used mainly for the lime sandstone industry but later proved very suitable for flower bulb cultivation. After 1950, the surface of bulb fields in almost 20 years was almost doubled by converting grassland into bulb ground. In recent years, many bulb farmers are starting to grow their bulbs in greenhouses.

Noordwijkerhout is about 5 kilometers from the North Sea. However, the village has no beach because the boundaries of Noordwijk have more or less enclosed the village. Yet, many people of Noordwijkerhout (in Dutch: Noordwijkerhouters) consider the Langevelderslag as their "beach" as they sing in their anthem. The Oosterduinsemeer, which Noordwijkerhouters call Lake Como, offers space for water recreation. The village has several campsites and hotels and there are many hiking and cycling routes in and around the village.
At the village centre of De Zilk you will find the entrance to the Amsterdam Waterleidingduinen. A beautiful dune area with the largest deer population in the Netherlands. In spring Noordwijkerhout and De Zilk are surrounded by colorful flower fields.

1 - Town Hall, Herenweg 4, Noordwijkerhout

The town hall of Noordwijkerhout was built in 1930 and has actually since then been used as a town hall. In 1956 the town hall was extended for the first time and in 1982 for a second time. After this second expansion, the reopening of the town hall in 1984 was done by Prince Bernhard of the Netherlands. The town hall used to have a few prison cells. On the west facade, just behind the platform, you can still see the heavily barred windows. The architect of the town hall in Noordwijkerhout, mr. Kropholler, is seen as the follower of architect H.P. Berlage. The architectural style is considered as that of the Delfste school. On the platform are sculptures of a bulb harvester and a bulb girl, symbols of the Noordwijkerhouts flower bulb company. On the tile picture above the platform is the municipal coat of arms of Noordwijkerhout, a standing yellow lion on a blue shield.

2 - Landhuis "De heerlijckheit Dyckenburch", Westeinde 82, Noordwijkerhout

The estate Dyckenburch is located on an old shoreline in the country estate zone between Noordwijk and Noordwijkerhout. On the west side the estate is surrounded by a dune area and the famous bulb fields. On the east side is the estate "Huize Remotus" and estate "Leeuwenhorst" with its parks and forests.

The estate Dyckenburch has a rich and moved history that is described in the book "The history of Dyckenburch" by dr. E. dan Hartog and drs. M. Bulting. The name "Dyckenburch" appears in 1721 for the first time. Over the centuries, the different residents have used different styles of writing. Until the Second World War, the Dyckenburch Estate was mainly privately inhabited by numerous prominent families. During the war, Dyckenburch was requisitioned by the German Wehrmacht. The house became the headquarters of the German commander. In 1945 the villa was taken into use as a Novitiate House. From 1951, after the departure of the fathers (priests), the villa was inhabited by repatriated Dutch from Indonesia. In 1962 the villa was converted into the famous and notorious campsite (and hotel) "Dijk en Burg". As a popular location for student corps, King Willem Alexander and his brothers spent their student days here. In 2000 the camp closed, after which the estate was bought by the current owner.

1

2

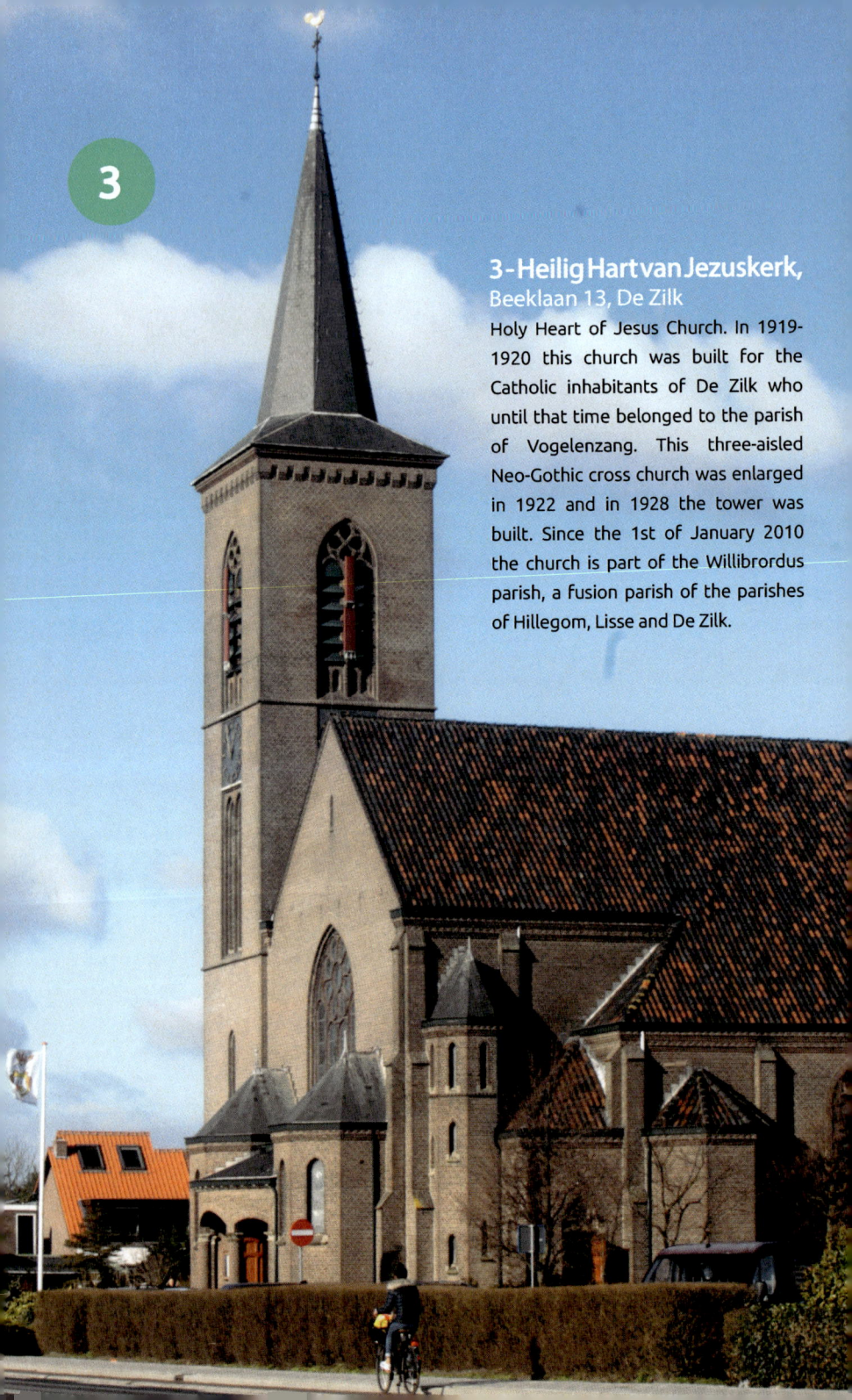

3

3 - Heilig Hart van Jezuskerk,
Beeklaan 13, De Zilk

Holy Heart of Jesus Church. In 1919-1920 this church was built for the Catholic inhabitants of De Zilk who until that time belonged to the parish of Vogelenzang. This three-aisled Neo-Gothic cross church was enlarged in 1922 and in 1928 the tower was built. Since the 1st of January 2010 the church is part of the Willibrordus parish, a fusion parish of the parishes of Hillegom, Lisse and De Zilk.

4

4 - Klein Leeuwenhorst, Gooweg 45, Noordwijkerhout

Klein Leeuwenhorst is a whitewashed neoclassical country house built in 1858. This house was sold in 1871 with a large piece of land. In 1872 a gardener's house was built on the Gooweg. In 1938 this house was given the name 'De Patrijs'. In the same year a stable and hunter's house were built. Huize Leeuwenhorst once stood on this estate from 1880. Both Huize Leeuwenhorst and the hunter's house were demolished in 1943 by order of the Wehrmacht for the construction of a tank ditch which was part of the Atlantic Wall. Klein Leeuwenhorst was requisitioned by the occupier during the war. After the Second World War the country house and the Stalhuis were renovated. Klein Leeuwenhorst and the Stalhuis are surrounded by 30 hectares of forest. The forest is open to the public. The Saddle room (Zadelkamer) in the Stalhuis is now used as a shop for decorative objects and when the store is closed the Saddle room can be rented. For more information, visit www.hetstalhuis.nl

5 - Koetshuis,
Gooweg 36, Noordwijkerhout

5

This carriage house is on the Nieuw Leeuwenhorst estate. On this estate used to be Huize Leeuwenhorst, a country house that the Gevers family had built in 1880-1882. In 1943 Huize Leeuwenhorst was demolished by order of the Wehrmacht for the construction of a tank ditch which was part of the Atlantic Wall. The carriage house has fortunately been saved.

6 - Sint Bavo, Langevelderweg 27, Noordwijkerhout

In 1913, the construction of the Sint Bavo was started. In 1915 the building was completed and inaugurated as a Roman Catholic psychiatric institution. The Sint Bavo was founded by the Congregation Brothers of Love (Congregatie Broeders van Liefde). The interior is set up with a symmetrical layout of eight pavilions and a few service buildings around the monastery and the chapel. This cruciform chapel is located at the back of the main building. Above the porch at the front is the statue of the Holy Bavo with the weapon of the Brothers of Love above it. Under the coat of arms on the tile picture is the text "Deus Caritas Est", God is Love. Because of the 25th anniversary of the establishment in 1939, the façade above the entrance was provided with a stone with the gold inscription "Psychiatric Institution St Bavo 1914-1939". Since 2005 the Sint Bavo is no longer in use. The building and the grounds have fallen prey to decay. There are now well-advanced plans for new construction on the Bavo site where the Bavo building, the Pesthuis (former barrack for infectious diseases) and house 't Hoogt (upbringing house) will be maintained.

7 - Sint Jozefkerk, Herenweg 13, Noordwijkerhout

This one-aisled cross church was built in 1916 and is part of the Sint Maarten parish. This originated on the 1st of January 2012 from a merger between the parish churches St. Jeroen and Maria ter Zee (Noordwijk), St. Jozef and St. Victor (Noordwijkerhout), St. Pancratius (Sassenheim), St. Matthias (Warmond) and St. Bartholomeus (Voorhout).

In the years 1964-1966 the church was rebuilt. The original Stations of the Cross, the pulpit, altars, benches and statues were then removed. In 2002 the interior has undergone a renovation in which part of the original interior and decoration could be brought back or restored. A Latin cross is built in the top of the west facade of the main room.

7

9

8 - Sint Victorkerk, Sint Victorlaan 13, Noordwijkerhout

The Sint Victorkerk would have arisen after the Reformation from a farm that served as a Clandestine church. In 1810 there was a church without a tower with a capacity of 250 seats. In 1851 it was decided to build a new church and in 1897 it was decided to expand. During the last renovation in 1938 the stone tower was added. The interior of the church was modernized in the 1960s. On the north side in the garden wall you can find three bricked rings, which used to be used for horses. The church is now part of the Parish Sint Maarten. This parish originated on the 1st of January 2012 from a merger between the parish churches St. Jeroen and Maria ter Zee (Noordwijk), St. Jozef and St. Victor (Noordwijkerhout), St. Pancratius (Sassenheim), St. Matthias (Warmond) and St. Bartolomeus (Voorhout).

9 - Witte Kerk, Dorpsstraat 7, Noordwijkerhout

Around the year 1300, the Witte Kerk (White Church) in Noordwijkerhout was built in Romanesque style. The church was dedicated to the apostles Paul and Peter and was used for Roman Catholic worship. In the year 1508 a gothic choir was added and the tower was raised. To prevent the church from falling into Spanish hands, it was set on fire by the Geuzen during the Siege of Leiden. Until 1618 the church remained as a ruin and church services were held in a school. Meanwhile, the church was assigned to the Reformed. It was not until 1620 that the ship of the church destroyed by the fire was restored. In 1975 the church was restored and in 1987 the church was expanded with a reconstruction of the 1573 destroyed gothic choir. The church is owned by the Protestant Municipality of Noordwijkerhout and the tower is owned by the civil municipality.

WHERE TO STAY
IN NOORDWIJKERHOUT

Hotel

NH Hotel Leeuwenhorst ★★★★
Langelaan 3
2211 XT Noordwijkerhout
Tel. 0252 - 378 888
www.nh-hotels.nl/hotel/nh-
noordwijk-conference-centre-
leeuwenhorst

Het Wapen van Noordwijkerhout
Dorpsstraat 14
2211 GC Noordwijkerhout
Tel. 0252 - 372 389
www.wapenvannoordwijkerhout.nl

Bed & Breakfast

Soete Inval
's-Gravendamseweg 43
2211 WH Noordwijkerhout
Tel. 0252 - 374 429
www.minihotelholland.nl

B&B The Cottage
De Vlashoven 2
2211 WL Noordwijkerhout
Tel. 0252 - 377 301

B&B Engelen aan Zee
Langevelderweg 91
2211 AE Noordwijkerhout
Tel. 06 - 42 87 95 93

B&B Halverwege
Delfweg 109
2211 VL Noordwijkerhout
Tel. 06 - 53 75 77 38

B&B Langeveld
Langevelderweg 145
2211 BL Noordwijkerhout
Tel. 06 - 23 36 60 99

B&B De Raetskamer
Schoolstraat 17 a/b
2111 AE Noordwijkerhout
Tel. 06 - 11 42 04 07
www.pensionderaetskamer.nl

B&B De Rotonde
's-Gravendamseweg 22
2211 WK Noordwijkerhout
Tel. 06 - 15 34 32 58
www.rotonde-noordwijkerhout.nl

B&B Tulpenzicht
Zilkerbinnenweg 14
2191 AC De Zilk
Tel. 0252 - 527 152
www.tulpenzicht.nl

Vakantiehuis Groenewege
Zeestraat 54
2211 XJ Noordwijkerhout
Tel. 06 - 53 29 03 24

Vakantiewoning Ruigenhoek
Ruigenhoek 13
2191 AG De Zilk
Tel. 06 - 28 18 87 71
www.vakantiewoning-ruigenhoek.nl

Zzz..

CAMPINGS/BUNGALOWS IN NOORDWIJKERHOUT

Bungalowpark Landal Dunimar
Ruigenhoekerweg 5
2211 ZG Noordwijkerhout
Tel. 0900 - 8842
www.landal.nl/parken/dunimar

Bungalow- & Caravanpark
De Wijde Blick
Schulpweg 60
2211 XM Noordwijkerhout
Tel. 0252 - 372 246
www.bungalowparkdewijdeblick.nl

Bungalowpark Sollasi
Duinschooten 12
2211 ZC Noordwijkerhout
Tel. 0252 - 374 460
www.sollasi.nl

Camping Sollasi
Duinschooten 14
2211 ZC Noordwijkerhout
Tel. 0252 - 376 437
www.sollasi.nl

Camping Op Hoop van Zegen
Westeinde 76
2211 XR Noordwijkerhout
Tel. 0252 - 375 491
www.campingophoopvanzegen.nl

RESTAURANTS IN NOORDWIJKERHOUT

Arthur (lunch)
Dorpsringweg 4
2211 ED Noordwijkerhout
Tel. 0252 - 372 673
www.lunchenbijarthur.nl

Como & Co
Boekhorsterweg 18
2211 AL Noordwijkerhout
Tel. 06 - 53 15 19 28
www.como-co.nl

Hillarey's
Leidsevaart 171
2211 WE Noordwijkerhout
Tel. 0252 - 377 787
www.hillareys.nl

Hudson Bar & Kitchen
Dorpsringweg 1
2211 ED Noordwijkerhout
Tel. 0252 - 740 100
www.restauranthudson.nl

Indian Restaurant Invitation
Duinschooten 12
2211 ZC Noordwijkerhout
Tel. 0252 - 371 087
www.india-invitation.nl

La Madonna
Leidsevaart 171a
2211 WE Noordwijkerhout
Tel. 0252 - 514 383
www.restaurantlamadonna.nl

To Me@t Bij de buren
Havenstraat 2
2211 EH Noordwijkerhout
Tel. 0252 - 346 274
www.tomeat.nl

De Ruigenhoek
Herenweg 444
2211 VJ Noordwijkerhout
Tel. 0252 - 372 435
www.deruigenhoek.nl

Tespelduyn
Tespellaan 53
2211 VT Noordwijkerhout
Tel. 0252 - 241 333
www.tespelduyn.nl

Het Wapen van Noordwijkerhout
Dorpsstraat 14
2211 GC Noordwijkerhout
Tel. 0252 - 372 389
www.wapenvannoordwijkerhout.nl

Wokrestaurant Flamingo Oriental
Langelaan 2A
2211 XT Noordwijkerhout
Tel. 0252 - 344 655
www.orientalnoordwijkerhout.nl

RESTAURANT IN DE ZILK

King's Garden
Regenvlietweg 22
2191 BC De Zilk
Tel. 0252 - 515 439
www.kingsgardendezilk.nl

Chinese cuisine	Dutch cuisine	Italian cuisine
Indian cuisine	American cuisine	French cuisine

Teylingen
Sassenheim, Voorhout and Warmond

On January 1st, 2006, the former municipalities of Voorhout, Sassenheim and Warmond merged into the Municipality of Teylingen. The name Teylingen is derived from Slot Teylingen, the ruin in the neighborhood of Teijlingen, near Sassenheim. Despite the merger, the three villages have clearly retained their own identity.

Voorhout is a village with about 15,000 inhabitants. In 1988, the village celebrated its 1000th anniversary. The former name of Voorhout is Foranholte, the second part of the name -holte (hout, in English: wood) is a reference to the dune area that has been very woody in the past. In the past, most inhabitants earned their money with flower bulb cultivation. Nowadays, this is only a small percentage of the inhabitants. Most people with a job now work outside the village limits. Voorhout is the birthplace of physician, botanist, physicist, chemist, philosopher, headmaster and professor Herman Boerhaave (1668-1738). At the heart of the village his childhood home is still standing, the Boerhaavehuis. Countess of Holland and Henegouwen, Jacoba of Bavaria (1401-1436) lived in the Castle Teylingen for several years. Also keeper Edwin van der Sar was born in Voorhout.

Sassenheim approximately has the same amount of inhabitants as Voorhout. The coastal strip where Sassenheim is located is one of the oldest inhabited parts of Holland. In the early Middle Ages, the population mainly consisted of Angles and Saxons, Germanic people who settled in the region. This may explain the name Sassenheim: home or residence of Saxons. Sassenheim has also flourished by the flower bulb cultivation, but as in Voorhout, only a few people in Sassenheim still work in the bulb industry. In the 17th and 18th century rich merchants built large mansions in Sassenheim. Along the main street of Sassenheim there are still some beautiful villas from that time. They also set up beautiful outdoor places like Huis ter Leede and the Oude Koningshuys. Sassenheim has evolved into an industrial and commuting municipality.

Warmond is a prosperous village with about 5,000 inhabitants located on an old beach at Kagerplassen. The beach wall runs parallel to the Leede which is connected to the Old Rhine through several channels. Along the Leede are the Herenstraat and the Dorpsstraat, which in turn are connected to each other by many small alleyways, also known as 'dammen' (In English: dams). The Polderland located on the east side of the Kagerplassen is only accessible via the water or via the territory of other neighboring municipalities. Warmond had six castles in the Middle Ages. Only the Huys te Warmont with the surrounding estate forest has been preserved. There are a number of old farms and special houses in the village. Around the Kagerplassen are several ancient mills. Before the bulb cultivation emerged in Warmond, the agricultural sector was the main source of income. Still a source of income and uncontestably popular in Warmond are the water sports. The Kagerplassen are of course very suitable for this purpose. Biologist and writer Maarten 't Hart lives in Warmond and painter Jan Steen (1626-1679) lived in Warmond.

1

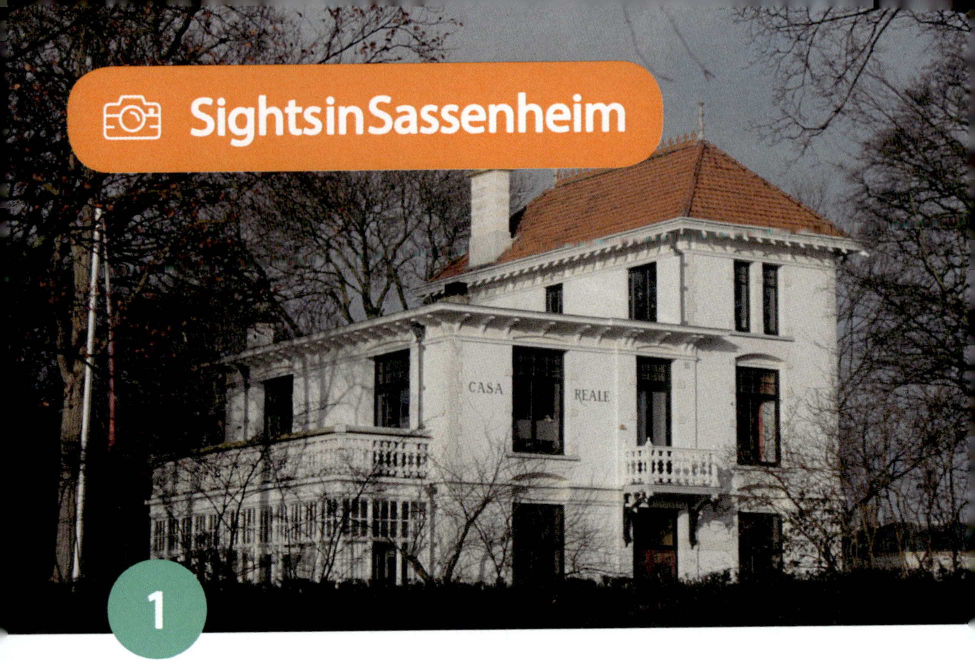

1 - Casa Reale, Hoofdweg 59, Sassenheim

The house was built in 1894 and is named after the Old Royal House (Oude Koningshuis) where the villa was once affiliated with. The house is built in a 'Transition style' with Italian influences.

2 - Dorpskerk,
Hoofdstraat 217, Sassenheim

The church was built in the 16th century. During the year of Leids Ontzet, 1574, the church was badly damaged by the Geuzen. In 1595 the church was renovated and in the year 1720 the church was enlarged. During restorations in the 70s, a typical Romanesque wall appears under the plaster layer, indicating that there was a Roman tuff brick ship, probably from the 12th century. The tower was probably built in the 13th century. The church is owned by the Protestant Church Sassenheim.

2

3 - Het Oude Koningshuys,
Wilhelminalaan 13-15, Sassenheim

Around the year 1628, the Oude Koningshuys (Old Royal House) was built by Johan van Nyenburgh. At that time the house was therefore known as 'Ter Nieuwburgh'. In 1680 it became the property of Stadholder-King Willem III. It is likely that the house owes its name to this time. Willem III never lived there himself. In the 18th century the house was also known as 'Sassigt'. Only the 17th century mansion and the 19th century carriage house have been preserved given by a beautiful park-like garden. The house is privately inhabited.

3

4

4 - Huis ter Leede, Ter Leedelaan 43, Sassenheim

This country estate was founded around 1660 by the Amsterdammer Nicolaas Dragon. It lies on the Ter Leedelaan on the north-east side of Sassenheim. Mr. Dragon lived in Huize Dever in Lisse for some time before he built this grand mansion. From 1928, Ter Leede was no longer permanently inhabited, but was used, among other things, as a training institute for the Catholic Guides Movement in the Netherlands. In 1981 the house has been restored and has since then been privately occupied again.

5 - Molen van Speelman, H. Knoopstraat 1, Sassenheim

In 1846 the mill was built by Jan Jacobus van Rhijn. Cornelis Johannes Speelman became owner in 1868. On October 29, 1868 the mill burned down by lightning. Even before the summer, the mill had already been rebuilt. Presumably the Amsterdam corn mill 'De Hoop' was used for this purpose. The superstructure of the mill was sold in 1882 for 1200 guilders and moved to De Cocksdorp on Texel where the mill burned down in 1920. Since 1993, the substructure has been owned by the 'De Molen van Sassenheim' foundation. The foundation has restored the mill in 1993-1994. The Molen van Speelman was once one of the largest windmills in the Dutch coastal region. There are plans to rebuild the mill in due time. Since November 2016 the Molen van Speelman has also been used as a wedding location. The mill can be visited when the blue pennant is blowing or else on request via:

www.demolenvansassenheim.nl

6

6 - Pancratiuskerk, Hoofdstraat 186, Sassenheim

A new church was built on the present site of this Roman Catholic church on 1870. This was a three-aisled Neo-Gothic church. After a few decades this church became too small and the current church was built in two phases. The transept and the priest's choir were built against the old church in 1913. In 1928 the old church was demolished and the new, larger ship and tower were built. Originally the village church of Sassenheim was dedicated to the holy Pancratius, but during the Reformation this church was transferred to the Protestants.

The Pancratiuskerk is part of the Parish Sint Maarten. This parish was formed on the 1st of January 2012 from a merger between the parish churches St. Jeroen and Maria ter Zee (Noordwijk), St. Jozef and St. Victor (Noordwijkerhout), St. Pancratius (Sassenheim), St. Matthias (Warmond) and St. Bartholomeus (Voorhout).

WHERE TO STAY IN SASSENHEIM

Z z z ..

Hotel
Hotel Sassenheim ★★★★
Warmonderweg 8
2171 AH Sassenheim
Tel. 0252 - 219 019
www.hotelsassenheim.nl

Bed & Breakfast
B&B The Orangerie
Baron van Heemstralaan 13
2172 JE Sassenheim
www.theorangerie.nl

RESTAURANTS IN SASSENHEIM

Brasserie Hemels (lunch)
Voorhavenkwartier 51
2171 HW Sassenheim
Tel. 0252 - 347 521
www.brasseriehemels.nl

Da Noi 🇮🇹
Hoofdstraat 167 A
2171 BB Sassenheim
Tel. 0252 - 752 688
www.ristorante-danoi.nl

De Voogd 🇫🇷
Hoofdstraat 267B
2171 BD Sassenheim
Tel. 0252 - 232 770
www.eetcafedevoogd.nl

Grand café Graaf Jan 🇳🇱
Jan Van Brabantweg 3
2171 HC Sassenheim
Tel. 0252 - 258 007
www.graaf-jan.nl

MacDonald's Sassenheim
(Fast food)
Stationslaan 1
2171 KW Sassenheim
Tel. 0252 - 220 655
www.mcdonaldsrestaurant.nl/
Sassenheim

Restaurant Nest 🇳🇱 🇫🇷
Warmonderweg 8
2171 AH Sassenheim
Tel. 0252 - 219 019
www.hotelsassenheim.nl/
eten-drinken

Op Eigen Wijze 🇳🇱
Hoofdstraat 265
2171 BD Sassenheim
Tel. 0252 - 865 411
www.opeigenwijze.info

OZZO Sushi & Lounge 🔲
Warmonderweg 8
2171 AH Sassenheim
Tel. 0252 - 219 019
www.sassenheim.ozzo.nl

Peking 🇨🇳
Parklaan 144-146
2171 EK Sassenheim
Tel. 0252 - 214 040
www.peking-sassenheim.nl

Vishandel Schuitemaker 🇳🇱 (fish)
Oude Haven 3
2171 GG Sassenheim
Tel. 0252 - 210 151
www.sild.nl

Chinese cuisine   Dutch cuisine

French cuisine   Italian cuisine

Japanese cuisine

1

1 - Boerhaavehuis, Kerkweg 11, Voorhout

In the green heart of Voorhout, a stone's throw from the Sint Bartholomeus church and the Kleine Kerk (Little Church), the Boerhaavehuis is home to the beautifully landscaped Boerhaavetuin (Boerhaave garden). The Boerhaave House was probably built around 1640 and has since become the residence of pastors of the Protestant Kleine Kerk in Voorhout. The current preacher is the 37th resident of the Boerhaavehuis. The entrance of the house is in the symmetry axis of the Boerhaavetuin. The house has a spacious marble corridor, vast attics and several living and sleeping rooms. In the largest living room there is another niche where reportedly the bedstead was in which Hermann Boerhaave would have been born on the 31st of December 1668.

The house has been restored and rebuilt several times over the centuries. When there was no money in 1957 to pay for a much-needed maintenance, a piece of land between the garden and the Churchillaan (the so-called Domineesbos) was sold to the municipality of Voorhout.

A group of volunteers takes care of the maintenance of the Boerhaavetuin every week. The Boerhaavehuis is not designed for public, but the garden is freely accessible from Monday to Saturday from 10 am to 4 pm and on Sunday from noon to 4 pm.

For more information
www.boerhaavehuis.nl

2

2 - Molen Hoop doet Leven,
along the Leidsevaart, corner 1e Elsgeesterweg, Voorhout

This polder mill originally stood in Rijnsburg and was used there for the drainage of the Kamphuizen polder. The mill is a so-called ground sailor. Because the expansion of the Flora flower auction meant that there was no room left for the mill in Rijnsburg, it was moved to the Elsgeest polder in 1999. The mill now operates in the Elsgeest polder on a voluntary basis and is owned by the Rijnlandse Molenstichting (Mill Foundation). The mill is usually open to visitors on Saturdays from noon to 3 pm.

3 - Teylingen Castle, Teylingerlaan 13-15, Voorhout

The Ruin of Teylingen is what remains of the 13th century Slot Teylingen. The lords of Teylingen, related to the house of the count, are mentioned for the first time in 1143. When in 1282 this family dies out in the male line, the castle falls to the countess. The Slot then takes on the function of forestry and hunting lodge.

The most famous inhabitant of the castle was the Dutch Countess Jacoba of Bavaria. During the Eighty Years' War, the castle was badly damaged. In 1572 it fell prey to the Spaniards during the siege of Haarlem and Leiden. What remains is a construction trap. After 1605, repairs are carried out and the castle is mainly used as a prison. In 1676 the residential tower burns out completely. In 1857, the ruin was acquired by two young van Teylingen during a public sale. In 1889 the castle was donated to the Kingdom.
At the end of the twentieth century, the ruin had been renovated and the canal, which had been partly filled up, was restored. Since the 1st of June 2013 the ruin has been managed by the Stichting Beheer Kasteel Teylingen (Management Foundation Castle Teylingen).

For information about visits and opening hours:
www.kasteelteylingen.nl

4 - Kleine Kerk,
Dr. Aletta Jacobslaan 9, Voorhout

The Kleine Kerk (Little Church) was built in the 14th century. The church stands on a high cemetery and consists for a large part of the tuff brick choir of the medieval village church. The ship of this village church was returned to the Catholics in 1809. The ship was separated from the Protestant part by a wall. After the tower was burnt by lightning, the Roman Catholic part was demolished and the Sint Bartholomeuskerk was built. Tombstones of the famous Voorhout family Boekhorst lie beneath the wooden floor in the church. At the cemetery next to the church is the morgue that is, like the church itself, a national monument. In 1913 the church had become too small and was expanded. The first stone was then laid by a 3.5 year old girl. In 1914 the enlarged church was festively used and in 1988 the church was renovated.

4

5 - Sint Bartholomeüskerk,

The Sint Bartholomeüskerk is located in the centre of Voorhout. This Neo-Gothic church is dedicated to the Apostle Bartholomeüs. The church was built in 1873 after the tower of the previous church was burnt down due to lightning. It took until 1881 before the Catholic part of the church and the tower were demolished and a new church was built.

During the Reformation a part of the church was appropriated by the Protestants. This part is still there and is now known as the Kleine Kerk. There is a cemetery on the side o f both churches. The part on the side of the Kleine Kerk is the Protestant cemetery. Next to the Bartholomeüskerk is the Catholic cemetery and also the municipal cemetery. In the Second World War the church narrowly escaped a British bombardment. The British thought that the occupying forces used the tower as a lookout. The bomb ended up in a backyard, between the current Herenstraat and Irenestraat. In 1973 the church was radically restored. In 2008 restoration work took place where the rooster disappeared from the tower. As a replacement, a tower rooster was placed that came from the Haagse Onze Lieve Vrouwe van Goede Raad-kerk. This church was completely destroyed in 1945 by a bombardment. In 2008, the missing rooster was found during groundwork on the Oosthoutlaan. Until 2008 there was a deep pond in front of the church. This has given way to a shallow basin with a fountain and on the bottom a mosaic image of the holy Bartholomeüs. On the east side of the church is the Boerhaavehuis. Since 2012 the church building is owned by the fusion parish Sint Maarten.

WHERE TO STAY
IN VOORHOUT

Hotel

Hotel Restaurant Boerhaave
Herenstraat 57
2215 KE Voorhout
Tel. 0252 - 211 483
www.boerhaave-voorhout.nl

Bed & Breakfast

B&B Pergamo
Loosterweg 14
2215 TM Voorhout
Tel. 06 - 15 45 73 54
www.bedandbreakfastpergamo.nl

B&B Wellness Lodge aan Zee
's Gravendamseweg 56
2215 TE Voorhout
Tel. 06 - 40 39 90 07

RESTAURANTS IN VOORHOUT

Asian Cuisine Oosthout
Oosthoutplein 15
2215 VM Voorhout
Tel. 0252 - 232 479

Het Alternatief
Herenstraat 62
2215KJ Voorhout
Tel. 0252 - 216 734
www.voorhout-alternatief.nl

Hotel Café Restaurant Boerhaave
Herenstraat 57
2215 KE Voorhout
Tel. 0252 - 211 483
www.boerhaave-voorhout.nl

Cheers !
Herenstraat 106
2215 KK Voorhout
Tel. 0252 - 231 525
www.cheersvoorhout.nl

Heren 52 (lunch)
Herenstraat 52
2215 KJ Voorhout
Tel. 0252 - 514 133
www.heren52.nl

Stef's & Jeff's (BBQ)
Herenstraat 74
2215 KJ Voorhout
Tel. 0252 - 866 550
www.stefsenjeffs.nl

Lunchroom Ons Genoegen (lunch)

Herenstraat 100

2215 KK Voorhout

Tel. 0252 - 235 748

www.lunchroomonsgenoegen.nl

Proeflokaal Sijgje

Jacoba van Beierenweg 150

2215 KX Voorhout

Tel. 0252 - 742 079

www.proeflokaalsijgje.nl

Café Welgelegen

Jacoba van Beierenweg 90

2215 KZ Voorhout

Tel. 0252 - 211 753

www.cafe-welgelegen.nl

Chinese cuisine

Dutch cuisine

French cuisine

SightsinWarmond

1 - Groot-Leerust, Burgemeester Ketelaarstraat 1, Warmond

The construction of the Groot-Leerust estate started in 1717. Since 1947 it has been the property of the municipality that opened the park in 1953 to the public and rented the house. In 1982 the house, which was then in poor condition, was sold. Behind the house is a park in landscape style with numerous trees. On the River the Leede there is a tea dome that would have been built around the year 1800. The wooden construction on stone plinth offers a magnificent view over the Leede and the polder landscape on the other side. There once lived the Governor General of the Dutch East Indies, Johannes Siberg and two mayors of Warmond. The house has been completely restored and is currently privately occupied.

2-DutchReformedChurch, Herenweg 82, Warmond

The church dates from the year 1875 and is the successor of the church which is now referred to as the Warmonder Ruïnekerk. The church is owned by the Protestant Municipality of Warmond.

3

3 - Huys te Warmont,
Burgemeester Ketelaarstraat 31, Warmond

This country estate hidden in the forests of Warmond dates back to the Middle Ages. In its present form it is a castle-like 18th century Baroque country house with classicist influences. In one of the towers is another clock from the year 1392 that bears the name Barbara. The house still has an original Louis XVI interior. From the Middle Ages it was inhabited by the High Fiefdom Warmond.The forest is also known as the 'Forest of Krantz', after the Krantz family, which from 1901 to 1960 was the owner of Huys in Warmont. The most famous resident was without doubt Johan Van Duvenvoirde. He was Admiral of Holland and the commander of the Geuzen. He inhabited the Huys in Spanish times and after the destruction of the Huys by the Spaniards after the siege of Leiden he had permission to rebuild the Huys with the stones of previously demolished Warmonds' monasteries. The house is privately inhabited and is not accessible to the public. You can make a beautiful forest walk in the woods that surround the estate of approx. 23 hectares.

For more information about the history:
www.huystewarmont.webs.com

4 - Sint Matthias church, Herenweg 76, Warmond

In 1859 the Sint Matthias church was built. Originally, the Warmond Catholics went to Church in Sassenheim. Because of the growing number and the distance came the demand for a private church. The floor plan of the church is similar to that of the original Sint Matthijskerk, of which only 'the Old Tower' is left. In 1954 the church was enlarged with the Jozefkapel (Jozef chapel) as day church, the (Mariakapel) Maria chapel, the doopkapel (baptistery) and the current sacristy and cellar. Since 2012, Sint Matthiaskerk is part of the Sint Maarten merged parish.

5 - Het Oude Raadhuis, Dorpsstraat 36, Warmond

The Old Town Hall was built in 1867 and was used as a town hall until 1930. In 1982 the Association Het Oude Raadhuis of Warmond was established with the aim of preserving the monument as a 'public space'. In 1994 the building was completely restored. The building is currently used as a gallery and as an official wedding location. Next to the Town Hall is the old village school that was built in 1861.

6

6 - Vroenhof, Herenweg 52, Warmond

In 1865, the Vroenhof outpost was built for the notary Johan de Crane to replace the Weltevreden house, which was demolished in 1863. In 1924 and 1930 lower side wings were added. It is a notary house in Eclectic style. The landscaped gardens in English landscape style contain remnants of a landscaped garden from before 1865. The largest part of the garden dates from 1865. The house is privately inhabited and the garden is not public.

7

7 - Tea dome Groot-Leerust,
Burgemeester Ketelaarstraat 1, Warmond

This characteristic tea dome dates back to the year 1817 and is located in the backyard of the Groot-Leerust country estate. The former garden is now Park Groot-Leerust and is freely accessible. Since the summer of 2016 it is possible to enjoy a cup of coffee or tea with a view on the Warmonder Leede on the terrace near the teahouse.

8 - Warmonder Ruin church, Klinkenberg, Warmond

An old certificate from the year 1063 shows that in the early days Warmond only owned a chapel. And that this was a daughter church of the Groene kerkje (Green Church) in Oegstgeest. It is likely that this chapel has been replaced by a tuff brick church in the 12th century which was later replaced by a brick church with a tower. The chapel and later also the church were dedicated to Saint Matthias.

To prevent the Spaniards from finding a safe haven in the church, it was destroyed by Leidenaren (People from Leiden) in 1573. The reformed later rebuilt the church and the tower. In 1874, when the reformed moved to the new church on the Herenweg, the choir was demolished. Only the Oude Toren (Old Tower) and the corresponding ruin have been preserved.

9 - Former house of Dutch painter Jan Steen,
Jan Steenlaan 36, Warmond

Jan Steen was a famous painter from Leiden who lived in Warmond from 1656 to 1660. One of his most famous paintings is the 'Household of Jan Steen'. In Dutch, 'Een huishouden van Jan Steen' has become a widely used saying. It indicates a messy interior. When Jan's wife died, he moved back to Leiden in 1669. There he lived the rest of his life in the house he inherited from his parents. Jan Steen died in 1679 and was buried in the family grave in the Pieterskerk in Leiden. Opposite the house is a bust of Jan Steen from 2008.

10 - Estate Oostergeest,
Laan van Oostergeest 1, Warmond

The Estate Oostergeest was built around 1650 and as is the case with many country estates, originated from a farm. The house is built in classicist style. In 1667 there was already a mansion and in 1729 more land was purchased, giving the estate the size it now has.

Originally, the garden of Oostergeest was geometrically designed, but from the beginning of the 19th century adjustments were made to a garden in landscape style. In the garden are still three gazebos from the 18th and 19th century. There is a stork's nest in the pasture in front of the house. For years the nest has been inhabited by breeding storks. During the Second World War the house was confiscated by the Germans. Some of the bunkers on the site still remind us of this time. The house is privately occupied. For 150 years, the house and the park have been owned by the same family.

11

11 - Mariënhaven, Mgr. Aengenentlaan 1, Warmond

In ancient times there were two convents in Warmond, a monastery, Mariënhaven founded in 1412 and a women's monastery, St. Ursula or Elfduizend Maagden (Eleven Thousand Virgins), founded in 1410. Both monasteries were founded by Jan van den Woude, Lord of Warmond. Mariënhaven stood on the spot where now the new housing estate Kloosterwei is located and St. Ursula stood on the spot just north of the current church ruin. In 1573 both monasteries were destroyed.

Until 1967, the large seminary of the Diocese of Haarlem was located in Warmond in the neoclassical seminary building with the same name as the former monastery; Mariënhaven. This seminary, founded in 1799, was the first Roman Catholic seminary in northern Netherlands. The corresponding chapel dates from 1843. In 1930 the seminary was extended with a new wing and a second chapel. Nowadays, the building serves as the nursing home of Marente.

WHERE TO STAY IN WARMOND

Bed & Breakfast

Kaag Resort
Veerpolder 1
2361 KV Warmond
Tel. 088 - 200 23 45
www.kaagresort.nl

Guesthouse Warmond
Herenweg 96
2361 EV Warmond

Kitty's Place Warmond
Wasbeeklaan 9
2361 HG Warmond

The Swann Inn
Haarlemmertrekvaart 1
2361 PB Warmond
Tel. 06 - 22 55 73 78

CAMPINGS IN WARMOND

Camping De Boekhorst
Boekhorsterweg 23 (via Oud Ade)
2362 AH Warmond
Tel. 071 - 501 86 23
www.campingdeboekhorst.nl

Camping Ducdalf
Oosteinde 15
2361 HB Warmond
Tel. 071 - 301 12 82
www.nederland-camping.nl/
camping/Warmond/Ducdalf/

Camping 't Haasje
Boekhorsterweg 22
2362 AH Warmond
Tel. 071 - 501 82 88
www.fietsenwandelweb.nl/poi/
view/47222701/Camping-t-Haasje.nl

Camping de Hof van Eeden
Hellegatspolder 2
2361 NA Warmond
Tel. 0252 - 212 573
www.dehofvaneeden.nl

Camping Horizon
Sweilandpolder 10a
2362 XC Warmond
Tel. 071- 501 85 03
www.nederland-camping.nl/
camping/Warmond/Horizon

Camping Kagerplassen
Scouting Camping ground,
Zijldijk 4
2362 AE Warmond
www.kagerplassen.scouting.nl

Camping Kagerzoom
Oosteinde 11 Warmond
Tel. 06 - 53 15 50 21
www.campingkagerzoom.nl

Camping Rianto
Oosteinde 11a
2361 HB Warmond
Tel. 071 - 301 04 86
www.rianto.nl

Jachthaven / Camping Spijkerboor
Boekhorsterweg 21
2362 AH Warmond
Tel. 071 - 501 88 69
www.campingspijkerboor.nl

Camping De Wasbeek
Wasbeeklaan 5b
2361 HG Warmond
Tel. 071 - 301 13 80
www.vekabo.nl/accommodaties/nl/
zuid-holland/teylingen/de-wasbeek

Camping - Jachthaven Zonnekamp
Oosteinde 9
2361 HA Warmond
Tel. 071 - 301 03 35
www.zonnekamp.com

RESTAURANTS IN WARMOND

Bistro La Croute 🟰 ▮▮
Dorpsstraat 114
2361 BP Warmond
Tel. 071 - 341 18 26
www.dezon-bistrolacroute.nl

Brasserie Stationskoffiehuis 🟰
Herenweg 1
2361 EA Warmond
Tel. 071 - 301 22 52
www.stationskoffiehuis.com

Brasserie de Kaagsociéteit 🟰
Sweilandpolder 8
2362 AG Warmond
Tel. 071 - 501 82 22
www.kaagsocieteit.nl

De Moerbei ▮▮ 1 Michelin Star
Dorpsstraat 5
2361 AK Warmond
Tel. 071 - 515 68 98
www.demoerbeiwarmond.nl

Het Paviljoen 🟰
Koudenhoorn 3 (On the recreation island) 2361 CP Warmond
Tel. 0252 - 860 423
www.paviljoenwarmond.nl

Het Wapen van Warmond 🟰
Dorpsstraat 90
2361 BK Warmond
Tel. 071 - 301 02 18
www.hetwapenvanwarmond.nl

Grand Cafe de Oude School
Dorpsstraat 38-40
2361 BE Warmond
Tel. 071 - 737 04 48
www.grandcafedeoudeschool.nl

Ristorante Pizzeria Caruso ▮▮
Burgemeester Nederburghlaan 12
2361 AJ Warmond
Tel. 071 - 301 33 31
www.pizzeria-caruso.nl

Timber Club 🟰
Veerpolder 20
2361KV Warmond
Tel. 071 - 305 88 88
www.dekkerwarmond.nl/php/timberclub.php

 Dutch cuisine ▮▮ Italian cuisine ▮▮ French cuisine

Keukenhof Gardens
Welcome to the Flower Paradise

Keukenhof can be reached within half an hour from The Hague, Haarlem, Leiden, Delft and Amsterdam.

7 million flower bulbs

Keukenhof is a park in which over 7 million flower bulbs are planted every year. The gardens of four pavilions show a fantastic collection of: Tulips, hyacinths, daffodils, orchids, roses, carnations, iris, lilies and many other flowers. You will be overwhelmed by the spectacle of colours and scents.

Directions and opening times

The Keukenhof is located in Lisse, between Amsterdam and The Hague, in the heart of the flower bulb-cultivation area, and can be easily reached via the A4 (exit Nieuw-Vennep) and the A44 (exit 3 Lisse). Follow the signs 'Keukenhof' from the exit. You can also reach the Keukenhof by public transport. The Keukenhof is surrounded by flowers everywhere. Distributed over different gardens and pavilions you will find millions of tulips and other flowers. Every year, the park is dominated by a new theme and therefore the Keukenhof is always different. A unique park that attracts more than one million visitors every year. Please note that the tulips only bloom from mid-March to mid-May, so the park is only open during this period. Daily from 8.00 -19.30.

Walks in Keukenhof between the tulips

The 15 km long hiking trail in the Keukenhof park offers a spectacular view of wonderfully fragrant tulips and greenhouses. The many restaurants with their large terraces invite you to take a break and enjoy the weekly flower exhibitions in peace and quiet. If you plan your visit with children, they have the possibility to participate in an exciting treasure hunt through the park area in the Keukenhof and/or to try out the large playground with a lot of fun.

The sculpture park in Keukenhof

In addition to the magnificent and large flower gardens, Keukenhof also has the largest sculpture park in the Netherlands, where over 150 sculptures by Dutch and international artists are on display.

Dutch souvenirs from Keukenhof

In the souvenir shop you can buy traditional and classic Dutch souvenirs. Whether as a gift or simply as a lasting memory. For example: the Dutch wooden shoes or the flower bulbs will give you a lot of pleasure!

Flower park Keukenhof - Tulip blossom holland

Imagine the following: over 34 hectares of fields planted with colourful tulips and hyacinths that shine in the spring sun. At Keukenhof, about 30 minutes from Amsterdam, this picture is a reality. Every autumn, a team of hardworking gardeners begin the sweaty task of planting about seven million bulbs. They proceed with precision that is almost reminiscent of art. The result a few months later speaks for itself. The Keukenhof, also known as 'Europe's garden', opens its gates every year between March and April for over 1,000,000 visitors.

There are many flowers to see, but the tulips are without doubt the stars of the Keukenhof. The accurately planned and laid out flower beds and meadows are embedded in a landscape of trees, sparkling lakes and fountains. The landscape is rounded off by a windmill, which should not be missing in Holland. Take your time to stroll through the park on the 15 km long paths.

Colourful tulip fields

The innumerable tulip rows extend beyond the park borders. A sight that is now quite normal for residents, but unique for the visitors of the Keukenhof. There are several ways to visit the fields. For example, you can rent bicycles and explore the surroundings around the park in comfort.

Alternatively, we recommend a canal cruise by boat. Cruise around the Keukenhof, the tulip fields and the idyllic Dutch countryside. The bird's-eye view is an attractive option for admiring the entire size of the park. Take a DC-3 Dakota plane for a journey through time and enjoy the beautiful nature at 450 meters above sea level. You will never forget this experience! www.dutchdakota.nl

Floral Events

Back on Earth you can visit various events in the park every weekend. Every year Keukenhof Park has a different motto on which the events are based. There are musical, cultural and culinary events. During the season there are over 30 flower exhibitions, each with different flowers and perennials.

Flower Parade - Bloemencorso van de Bollenstreek

The highlight of the year is the flower parade (Bloemencorso) Annually on the first Saturday after April 19. The move takes place over a 40 km long route through the neighbouring villages of Noordwijk and Haarlem. Of course, the flowers are the main attraction of the parade. Regardless of its shape or size, every van is decorated with luxurious floral arrangements. For all information on this event: www.bloemencorso-bollenstreek.nl

Keukenhof Stationsweg 166A 2161 AM Lisse
www.keukenhof.nl

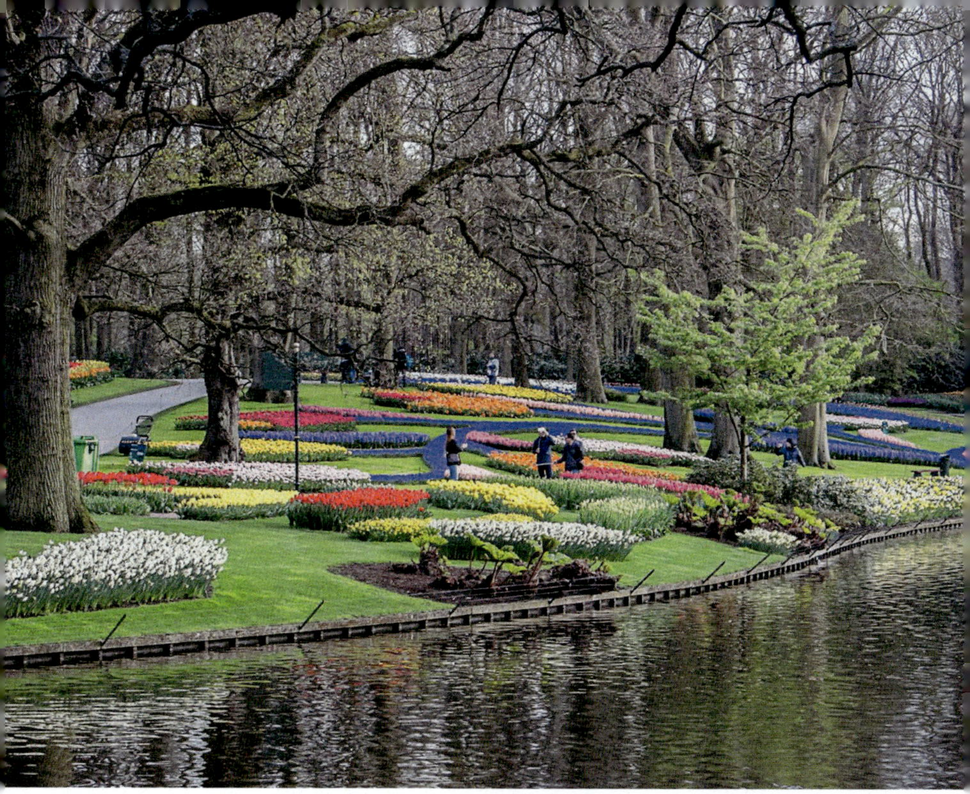

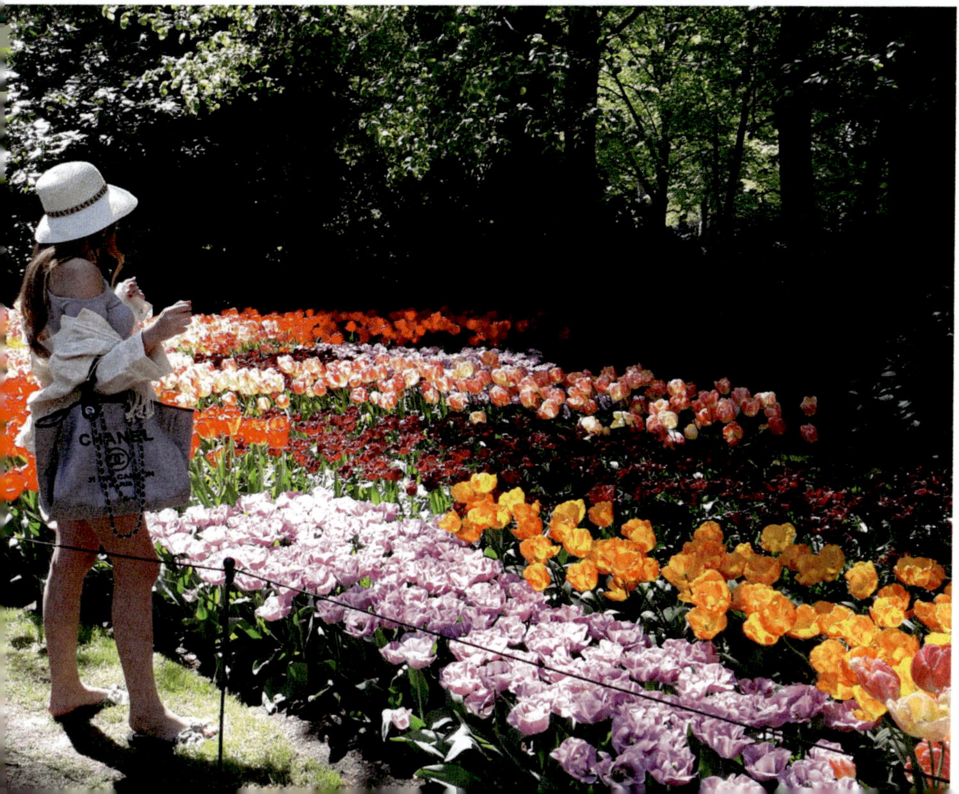
CHANEL

ACTIVITIES FOR CHILDREN

HILLEGOM

Paintball & Lasergame Leidsestraat 187 2182 DM Hillegom
Tel. 06 - 55 38 65 44 www.paintballhillegom.nl

Playground Weerestein Michiel de Ruijterstraat 95 2182 XM Hillegom
Tel. 0252 - 522 037 www.weerestein.nl

Playground Kindervreugd Prinses Marijkestraat 67 2181 RN Hillegom
Tel. 0252 - 522 028 www.kindervreugdhillegom.nl

KATWIJK

Lasergame Sports Katwijk Sandtlaan 54 2223 GG Katwijk
Tel. 071 - 202 00 07 www.lasergamenkatwijk.nl

LISSE

Playground Marijke Crocussenstraat 3A 2161 HV Lisse
www.svmarijke.nl

Petting Zoo Poelepetaat Kasteel Keukenhof Keukenhof 1 2161 AN
Lisse www.kasteelkeukenhof.nl/nl/ontdek-het-landgoed/kinderboerderij

NOORDWIJK

Jumping Noordwijk Indoor Trampolinepark Van Berckelweg 34
2203 LB Noordwijk Tel. 071 - 303 15 57 www.jumpinnoordwijk.nl

Rollygolf Noordwijk Midgetgolf / Trampolines / Minicars
Duinweg 6 2202 ZN Noordwijk Tel. 071 - 361 31 29 www.derollygolf.nl

Space Expo Noordwijk Keplerlaan 3 2201 AZ Noordwijk
Tel. 071 - 364 64 48 www.space-expo.nl

NOORDWIJKERHOUT

Petting Zoo de Dierenhoeve Langevelderweg 27 2211 AB
Noordwijkerhout Tel. 06 - 18 53 61 49 http://www.dierenhoeve.nl

Playground De Speelakker Zeereep 1 2211 EL Noordwijkerhout
Tel. 0252 - 372 832 www.speelakker.nl

Kids Zoo Indoor Playground Pletterij 3 2211 JT Noordwijkerhout
Tel. 0252 - 372 626 www.kidszoo.nl

RIJNSBURG

Quad Riding Marina Rijnsburg Kanaalpad NW 4 2231 NX Rijnsburg
Tel. 071 - 407 96 82 www.marinarijnsburg.nl/quad-rijden

Kids Paintball Marina Rijnsburg Kanaalpad NW 4 2231 NX Rijnsburg
Tel. 071 - 407 96 82 www.marinarijnsburg.nl/paintball

SASSENHEIM

Playground Bijdorp Krelagehove 2 2172 VE Sassenheim
www.sites.google.com/site/bijdorp20

Playground DVV Sporthofflaan 26-28 2172 BR Sassenheim
www.speeltuinverenigingdvv.nl

VALKENBURG ZH

Steam Train Katwijk Leiden Pellenbargweg 1 2235 SP Valkenburg ZH
Tel. 071 - 572 42 75 www.stoomtreinkatwijkleiden.nl

WARMOND

Farmer's Golf / Canoeing Wasbeeklaan 31 2361 HG Warmond
Tel. 0252 - 230 083 www.boerengolfvandergeest.nl

Monkey Town Indoor Playground Veerpolder 15c 2361 KX Warmond
Tel. 071 - 362 74 42 www.monkeytown.eu/warmond

Jump XL Warmond Veerpolder 12 2361 KV Warmond
Tel. 071 - 301 82 49 www.jump-xl.com/nl/warmond

BICYCLE, SOLEX & VESPA RENT

LISSE

Rent-a-bike Van Dam
(location Keukenhof during opening hours Keukenhof)
Parking Head Entrance Keukenhof Stationsweg 166A 2161 AM Lisse
Tel. 06 - 12 08 98 58 www.rentabikevandam.nl

Bike Mobile Lisse De Nachtegaal Heereweg 10 2161 AG Lisse
Tel. 010 - 300 78 46 www.bimbimbikes.nl

Bike Mobile Lisse De Engel Heereweg 386 2161 DG Lisse
Tel. 010 - 300 78 46 www.bimbimbikes.nl

NOORDWIJK

Bicycle rent Noordwijk Duindamseweg 6 2204 AS Noordwijk
Tel. 0252 - 371 726 www.fietsverhuur-noordwijk.nl/nl/

Kees Fietsshop Van Speykstraat 4 2202 GK Noordwijk
Tel. 071 - 362 03 47 www.keesfietsshop.nl

NOORDWIJKERHOUT

Rent-a-bike Van Dam (location Noordwijkerhout) Havenstraat 22 2211EH
Noordwijkerhout Tel. 0252 - 372 482 www.rentabikevandam.nl

SASSENHEIM

Fietsverhuur (bike rent) Sassenheim Hoofdstraat 144
2171 BK Sassenheim Tel. 0252 - 211 127 www.profiledefietsspecialist.nl

Solex Verhuur Bollenstreek (Solex rent)
Have fun Events Jacoba van Beierenweg 97 A 2215 KW Voorhout
Tel. 085 - 487 44 00 www.solexverhuurbollenstreek.nl

Vespa Verhuur Noordwijk (Vespa rent)
Kabeljauwsteeg 1 2202 GA Noordwijk aan zee
Tel. 06 - 43 43 10 68 www.vespaverhuurnoordwijk.nl

 # BOWLING

All American Bowling
Langelaan 2 2211 XT Noordwijkerhout
Tel. 0252 - 372 202
www.allamericanbowling.nl

De Oude Tol Partycentrum
Hoofdstraat 147 2171 BA Sassenheim
Tel. 0252 - 216 850 www.oudetol.nl

 # CASINO

Casino - Hotel de Nachtegaal Heereweg 10 2161 AG Lisse
Tel. 0252 - 433 030 www.nachtegaal.nl/casino

Flamingo Casino Langelaan 2 2211 XT Noordwijkerhout
Tel. 0252 - 344 655 www.flamingocasino.nl/vestigingen/Noordwijkerhout/

Jack's Casino Warmonderweg 8 2171 AH Sassenheim Tel. 0252 - 220 300
www.jackscasino.nl/vestigingen/sassenheim

Flash Casino's Sassenheim Rijksstraatweg 61 2171 AL Sassenheim
Tel: 0252 - 227 389 www.flashcasinos.nl/casino-s/sassenheim

 # ELECTRIC CAR GPS TOURS

RENZY.NL Electric tours & rentals Meer en Duin 36 2163 HC Lisse
Tel. 0252 - 514 062 www.renzy.nl

ELECTRIC CAR GPS TOURS

FARM TOURS
FLOWERPICKINGGARDENS

Cheese Farm De Annahoeve Menneweg 42 2172 HE Sassenheim
Tel. 0252 - 213 018 www.deannahoeve.nl

FAM Flower Farm Heereweg 361 2161 CB Lisse
Tel. 0252 - 211 462 www.famflowerfarm.nl

Flower Farm De Tulperij Oude Herenweg 16B 2215 RZ Voorhout
Tel. 0252 - 228 720 www.detulperij.nl

Annemieke's Picking Garden Haarlemmerstraat 15a 2182 HA Hillegom
Tel. 06 - 53 83 99 79 www.annemiekespluktuin.nl

De Bollenburcht Teylingerlaan 13 2215 RT Voorhout
Tel. 0252 - 225 031 www.bollenburcht.nl

GALLERIES & ATELIERS

LISSE

Atelier Dircke Heereweg 467 2161 DC Lisse
Tel. 0252 - 520 547 www.dircke.nl

PLAN 4 Iet langeveld & Wout Ruigrok Heereweg 249 2161 BH Lisse
Tel. 06 - 40 08 46 14 www.ietlangeveld.nl - www.divertissimo.com

Galerie 'Het Grachthuisje' Kanaalstraat 39 2161 JB Lisse
Tel. 0252 - 412 950 www.grachthuisje.nl

Galerie Het Heerenhuis Heereweg 137 2161 BA Lisse
Tel. 06 - 20 23 78 03 www.galeriehetheerenhuis.nl

KATWIJK

Duna Atelier Boulevard 73 2225 HA Katwijk
Tel. 06 - 17 21 02 02 www.schilderenaanzee.nl

Kuco Kunst Atelier Katwijk Aan Zee
Noordzeepassage 103 2225 CD Katwijk www.kuco.nl

Galerie de Kunstberg Achterweg 12 2223 BE Katwijk aan den Rijn
Tel. 071 - 517 04 08 www.kunstberg.nl

Art Galerie Kraijenoord Prinses Marijkelaan 21 2224 VA Katwijk ZH
Tel. 071 - 401 35 20 www.inenomdehaagseschool.nl

NOORDWIJK

Artboutique Hogeweg 55 2201 AN Noordwijk
Tel. 071 - 361 87 54 www.artboutique.nl/bezoek-en-contact/exposities

Atelier Bannink & Co Goohorstlaan 10b 2203 BC Noordwijk
Tel. 071 - 361 55 02 www.atelierbannink-en-co.nl/contact-en-locatie

Galerie Klooster Hoofdstraat 96 2202 EZ Noordwijk
Tel. 071 - 361 09 30 www.kloosterevenementen.nl

RV Galerie & Atelier Van Limburg Stirumstraat 17 2201 JM Noordwijk
Tel. 06 - 24 95 47 72 www.rianverbeek.com/exposities

WARMOND

Art & Design Nicoline Heemskerk Veerpolder 59 2361 KZ Warmond
Tel. 071 - 301 26 20 www.nicoline-heemskerk.com

Galerie de Pomp Dorpsstraat 38 2361 BE Warmond
Tel. 071 - 301 11 09 www.galeriedepomp.nl

Galerie Het Oude Raadhuis Dorpsstraat 36 2361 BE Warmond
Tel. 071 - 301 03 81 www.hetouderaadhuisvanwarmond.nl

Atelier Margareth Meulmeester Dorpsstraat 85 2361 BA Warmond
Tel. 06 - 51 50 62 39 www.margarethmeulmeester.nl

VALKENBURG ZH

Atelier Het Souterrain Katwijkerweg 47 2235 AB Valkenburg Z-H
Tel. 071 - 407 34 10 www.atelierhetsouterrain.nl

VOORHOUT

Atelier / Galerie Yvonne Oosterwijk Engelselaan 49 2215 RJ Voorhout
Tel. 06 - 11 95 40 52 www.yvonneoosterwijk.nl

De Bollenburcht Teylingerlaan 13 2215 RT Voorhout
Tel. 0252 - 225 031 www.bollenburcht.nl

GOLF COURSES

Golfclub Ter Specke Spekkelaan 1 2161 GH Lisse
www.golfbaanterspecke.nl

Golfclub De Vijf Margen / Golfcentrum Noordwijk
Van Berckelweg 38 2202 LB Noordwijk Tel. 071 - 361 34 99
www.devijfmargen.nl - www.golfcentrumnoordwijk.nl

De Noordwijkse Golfclub Randweg 25 2204 AL Noordwijk
Tel. 071 - 373 764 www.noordwijksegolfclub.nl

Landgoed Tespelduyn Tespellaan 53 2211 VT Noordwijkerhout
Tel. 0252 - 241 333 www.tespelduyn.nl

Golfclub Kagerzoom Veerpolder 20 2361 KV Warmond
Tel. 071 - 576 82 14 www.kagerzoom.nl

HELICOPTER FLIGHTS & GLIDING

Helicopter flights / Have Fun Events Jacoba van Beierenweg 97 A
2215 KW Voorhout Tel. 085 - 487 44 00 www.havefunevents.nl/helikopter

KZC - Kennemer Zweefvlieg Club Vogelaardreef 21
2204 AA Noordwijk Tel. 0252 - 373 403 www.kzc.nl

HORSE RIDING

Manege Jonker Noordduinseweg 7 2221 BL Katwijk aan Zee
Tel. 071 - 402 47 43 www.manegejonker.nl

Manege 't Langeveld Langevelderlaan 39 2204 BC Noordwijk
Tel. 0252 - 375 429 www.sollasi.nl/manege/home/

Managerecreatie De Stal Duindamseweg 20 2204 AS Noordwijk aan Zee
Tel. 06 - 42 92 35 45 www.managerecreatie.com

Manege Bakker Schulpweg 62 2211 XM Noordwijkerhout
Tel. 0252 - 372 628 www.manege.nl

INDOORSKIING

Skicentrum Hillegom Vosselaan156 2821 CD Hillegom
Tel. 0252 - 527 120 www.skicentrumhillegom.nl

Skicentrum Sassenheim Wasbeekerlaan 24C 2171 AE Sassenheim
Tel. 0252 - 222 555 www.skicentrumsassenheim.nl

MARINAS

Jachthaven Katwijk Haringkade 6 2224 RA Katwijk
Tel. 071 - 402 97 93 www.jachthavenkatwijk.nl

Jachthaven Van der Meer 3e Poellaan 103 2161 DL Lisse
Tel. 0252 - 212 410 www.jachthavenvandermeer.nl

WSV Lisse Jachthavendam 2 2162 CT Lisse
Tel. 06 - 42 41 29 54 www.wsvlisse.nl/de-haven

Jachthaven Noordwijk Van Berckelweg 42 2203 LB Noordwijk
Tel. 06 - 42 13 97 19 www.jachthaven-noordwijk.nl

Marina Rijnsburg Kanaalpad NW 4 2231 NX Rijnsburg
Tel. 071 - 407 96 82 www.marinarijnsburg.nl

Jachthaven Jonkman Jachthaven 1 2172 JX Sassenheim
Tel. 0252 - 211 583 www.jachthavenjonkman.nl

Fort Marina Burg. Ketelaarstraat 7 2361 AA Warmond
Tel. 071 - 301 92 05 www.fortmarina.nl

Jachthaven Warmond Wasbeeklaan 31 2361 HG WARMOND
Tel. 0252 - 230 083 www.jachthavenwarmond.nl

Jachthaven Lockhorst Sweilandstraat 7a 2361 JA Warmond
Tel. 071 - 301 03 78 www.lockhorst.nl

Jachthaven Zwanengat Haarlemmertrekvaart 1 2361 PB Warmond
Tel. 071 - 523 70 45 www.jachthavenzwanengat.nl

Jachthaven Zonnekamp Oosteinde 9 2361 HA Warmond
Tel. 071 - 301 03 35 www.zonnekamp.com

Jachthaven Spijkerboor Boekhorsterweg 21 2362 AH Warmond
Tel. 071 - 501 88 69 www.campingspijkerboor.nl/watersport/jachthaven

 # MUSEUMS

KATWIJK

Katwijks Museum Voorstraat 46 2225 ER Katwijk
Tel. 071 - 401 30 47 www.katwijksmuseum.nl

Smalspoormuseum - Stoomtrein (steam train) Katwijk Leiden
Pellenbargweg 1 2235 SP Valkenburg ZH
Tel. 071 - 572 42 75 www.stoomtreinkatwijkleiden.nl

LISSE

Lisser Art Museum Keukenhof 14 2161 AN Lisse
www.lamlisse.nl

Museum De Zwarte Tulp Grachtweg 2A 2161 HN Lisse
Tel. 0252 - 417 900 www.museumdezwartetulp.nl

NOORDWIJK

Atlantic Wall Museum Bosweg (after 250m on the left of the cycle path)
2202 NX Noordwijk Tel. 071 - 361 57 85 www.atlantikwall.nl

Museum Engelandvaarders (war museum) Bosweg 15 2202 NX Noordwijk
Tel. 071 - 361 97 73 www.museumengelandvaarders.nl

Museum Noordwijk Jan Kroonsplein 4 2202 JC Noordwijk
Tel. 071 - 361 78 84 www.museumnoordwijk.nl

Space Expo Noordwijk Keplerlaan 3 2201 AZ Noordwijk
Tel. 071 - 364 64 89 www.space-expo.nl

Streekmuseum Veldzicht Herenweg 114 2201 AL Noordwijk
Tel. 06 - 42 20 45 46 www.streekmuseumveldzicht.nl

Toren Oude Jeroenskerk (climb the church tower)
Voorstraat 44 2201 HW Noordwijk
www.erfgoednoordwijk.nl/evenementen/torenklimmen-jeroenskerk-2

RIJNSBURG

Museum Oud Rijnsburg Oude Vlietweg 6 2231 CN Rijnsburg
Tel. 071 - 402 29 61 www.genootschapoudrijnsburg.nl

Museum Het Spinozahuis (Spinoza's house) Spinozalaan 29
2231SG Rijnsburg Tel. 071-402 92 09 www.spinozahuis.nl

VALKENBURG ZH

Torenmuseum (tower museum) Castellumplein 1a
2235 CN Valkenburg ZH Tel. 071-407 54 60 www.oudvalkenburgzh.nl

PAINTBALL & QUADS

Paintball & Lasergame Leidsestraat 187 2182 DM Hillegom
Tel. 06 - 55 38 65 44 www.paintballhillegom.nl

Quad Driving Marina Rijnsburg Kanaalpad NW 4 2231 NX Rijnsburg
Tel. 071 - 407 96 82 www.marinarijnsburg.nl/quads
Age 10 > and minimum of 8 participants

Paintball / Kidspaintball Marina Rijnsburg Kanaalpad NW 4
2231 NX Rijnsburg Tel. 071 - 407 96 82 www.marinarijnsburg.nl/paintball
Age 8 > and minimum of 8 participants

ROUND TRIPS & BOAT RENTAL

Rederij Van Hulst (round trips) Burg. Ketelaarstraat 42a 2361 AE
Warmond Tel. 071 - 301 01 33 www.rederijvanhulst.nl/afvaartlocaties

Rondvaart Katwijk (round trips) Haven 8 2225 BH Katwijk
Tel. 071 - 401 25 03 www.rondvaartbootkatwijk.nl

Marina Rijnsburg (boat rental) Kanaalpad NW 4 2231 NX Rijnsburg
Tel. 071 - 407 96 82 www.marinarijnsburg.nl/sloep-huren

Rederij Van Hulst (boat rental) Burg. Ketelaarstraat 42a 2361 AE
Warmond Tel. 071 - 301 01 33 www.rederijvanhulst.nl/sloepverhuur

Olympia Charters (boat rental) Veerpolder 61-67 2361 KZ Warmond
Tel. 071 - 301 00 43 www.olympia-charters.nl

SWIMMING POOLS

Outdoor Swimming Pool de Vosse (Apr-Sept) Vosselaan 152
2181 CD Hillegom Tel. 0252 - 519 001 www.devosse.nl

Swimming Pool Acquamar Sportbedrijf Katwijk Piet Heinlaan 5
2224 SW Katwijk Tel. 071 - 401 59 47
www.sportbedrijfkatwijk.nl/foto-album/zwembad-aquamar

Swimming Pool de Waterkanten Sportlaan 21 2161 VA Lisse
Tel. 0252 - 414 488 www.sportfondsenlisse.nl

Beach Hotel Noordwijk Koningin Wilhelmina Boulevard 31
2202 GW Noordwijk Tel. 071 - 367 68 77
www.beachhotelnoordwijk.nl/zwembad-noordwijk/zwembad-noordwijk

Swimming Pool Binnenzee Nieuwe Zeeweg 165 2202 HA Noordwijk
Tel. 071 - 361 33 33 www.binnenzee.com

De Schelft Maandagsewetering 202 2211 WV Noordwijkerhout
Tel. 0252 - 376 241 www.optisport.nl/schelft

Swimming Pool Wasbeek Van Alkemadelaan 12 2171 DH Sassenheim
Tel. 0252 - 215 594 www.stiwa.nl

THEATER, MUSICAL & CINEMA

TheaterHangaar (Musical - Soldier of Orange)
1e Mientlaan/Wassenaarseweg 75 2223 LA Katwijk
Tel. 071 - 401 45 11 www.theaterhangaar.nl

Theater Floralis / Bioscoop Floralisplein 69 2161 HX Lisse
Tel. 06 - 12 79 52 31 www.theaterfloralis.nl - www.cinemafloralis.nl

Theater De Muze / Cinema Wantveld 2 2202 NS Noordwijk
Tel. 071 - 364 62 26
www.demuzenoordwijk.nl

Zeep aan Zee - Theaterhouse
Voorstraat 14
2201 HV Noordwijk
www.zeepaanzee.nl

Theater Het Onderdak
J.P. Gouverneurslaan 40A
2171 ER Sassenheim
Tel. 0252 - 225 874
www.hetonderdak.nl

Classic Jazz Concert Club
(Partycentre de Oude Tol)
Hoofdstraat 157
2171 BB Sassenheim
www.classicjazzconcertclub.nl

De Muze

**Mimiekstheater (mime
theatre)** Kerkweg 3 2235 BC
Valkenburg ZH
www.mimiekstheater.nl

Theater Het Trefpunt Herenweg 80 2361 ET Warmond
www.theaterhettrefpunt.nl

WATER SPORTS

KATWIJK

AquaSports Parasailing, flyboarding, wakeboarding, tuberiding, rafting and more. Strandvak 23 north of Beachclub Wantveld Noordduinseweg 6 2221 BL Katwijk Tel. 06 - 53 78 17 33 www.aquasports.nl

Airtime Katwijk Kitesurfing Strandvak 23 north of Beachclub Wantveld Noordduinseweg 6 2221 BL Katwijk www.airtimekatwijk.nl

Flyboard Katwijk Flyboarding, hoverboarding, rib boats. Strandvak 23 north of Beachclub Wantveld Noordduinseweg 6 2221 BL Katwijk Tel. 06 - 53 78 17 33 www.flyboardkatwijk.nl

Katwijkse Branding Surfclub Windsurfing, kitesurfing, golfsurfing & supping. Strandvak 5, near the Katwijk lighthouse. Tel. 071 - 401 03 87 www.kbs.nl

NOORDWIJK

Beach Break Noordwijk Kiting, surfing, SUP's and Kayaks. Zeereep 106 Afrit (exit) 21 Noordwijk Tel. 06 - 19 67 32 27 www.beachbreak.nl

KSN Noordwijk Supping, kiting, skimboarding, bodyboarding, wakeboarding and windsurfing. Kon. Astrid Boulevard 103, 2202 BD Noordwijk Tel. 071 - 737 01 43 www.ksnoordwijk.nl

 **WELLNESS**

Azzurro Wellness Oude Zeeweg 57 2202 CJ Noordwijk
Tel. 071 - 361 22 21 www.azzurrowellness.nl

MC Wellness Koningin Astrid Boulevard 5 2202 BK Noordwijk
Tel. 071 - 365 13 45 www.mc-solution.nl

Hotel van Oranje Spa & Wellness Koningin Wilhelmina Boulevard
20 2202 GV Noordwijk Tel. 071 - 367 68 69
www.hotelvanoranje.nl/spa-en-wellness-aan-het-strand

Palace Wellness Centre
Pickeplein 8 2202 CL Noordwijk Tel. 071 - 365 30 00
www.radissonblu.com/en/palacehotel-noordwijk/wellness

Hotel Sassenheim-Leiden
Warmonderweg 8 2171 AH Sassenheim Tel. 0252 - 219 019
www.hotelsassenheim.nl/arrangementen/wellness-arrangement

Sauna Warmond Veerpolder 4 2361 KV Warmond
Tel. 071 - 301 19 76 www.saunawarmond.nl

PARKS, FORESTS & RECREATION

Adoptthepaceofnature,hersecretispatience-RalphWaldoEmerson

The stunning flower fields are not the only symbols of nature in the Dutch Flower Region. There is so much more to explore.

Dunes

In De Zilk you will find one of the entrances to the **Amsterdamse Waterleidingduinen**. A beautiful dune area with the largest deer population in the Netherlands. The dunes of Noordwijk and Katwijk are challenging you to go walking or cycling while enjoying being outdoors inhaling the air, taking in the scenery, snapping a few photos and discovering the diversity of nature.

Forests

If you like to go for a stroll in the forest there is the '**Pan van Persijn**' or '**Panbos**' in Katwijk. Entrance: Wassenaarseweg 152, 2223 LA Katwijk aan Zee.

The forest belonging to the **Landgoed Nieuw Leeuwenhorst** in Noordwijkerhout is another beautiful area worth visiting. It is part of the Nationaal Park Hollandse Duinen. The entrance is at Gooweg 36, 2211 XX Noordwijkerhout.

To the south of Keukenhof Gardens you will find Keukenhof Castle which is surrounded by the **Keukenhofbosch**, a varied and hilly woodland with beech, oak and pine trees. Keukenhof 1, 2161 AN Lisse.

The '**Bos van Krantz**' (Krantz' forest) is the 23 hectares forestal area surrounding the beautiful and historical Huys te Warmont Estate in Warmond. Herenweg 141, 2361 EP Warmond.

Noordwijk '**Landgoed Offem**' (Offem Estate) in Noordwijk is known for its old beech trees, oak trees, lawns and ponds. Offem is a private estate and not accessible. From the roads around the estate one gets a good impression, especially from the Nachtegaallaan on the east side.

Parks

A smaller forestal area with a beautiful pond and paths all around is the **Park Overbosch** in Voorhout. Entrance: Rijnsburgerweg 3, 2215 RA Voorhout. In Sassenheim **Park Rusthoff** is like a green oasis in the heart of Sassenheim just off the main shopping street. Little children will certainly enjoy the little petting zoo in this park. Entrance: Hoofdstraat, Sassenheim.

Recreational waters

One of the recreational lakes of the Dutch Flower Region is the **Valkenburgse meer** (lake of Valkenburg), J. Pellenbargweg, 2235 SP Valkenburg. You can take a ride with a steam train around the lake on the narrow-gauge Railway (smalspoorlijn) from Ascension Day until the last weekend of September. Another recreational lake is the **Oosterduinse meer** or Lake Como as the people from Noordwijkerhout call it. In summertime you can enjoy open water swimming in the Oosterduinse meer. Boekhorsterweg 18, 2211 AL Noordwijkerhout.

Warmond is home to the **Kagerplassen**. A small system of lakes to the northeast of the city of Leiden. Especially in summertime the Kagerplassen are a very popular area for boating, watersports, fishing, camping and walking. It can be very busy on hot summer days but definitely worth visiting. Rent a boat and enjoy the beautiful Dutch scenery of windmills and waterfront pasture land with grazing animals, flower fields, Dutch boats and yachts. A number of cycling, walking and mountainbiking routes can be found on www.bollenstreek-reisgids.nl (see section Activities) or go to one of the various Tourism offices (Dutch: VVV kantoren) in the Flower Region.

Oosterdui
Meer

N2

Noordwijkerhout

Noordwijk
aan Zee

N206

Noordwijk-
Binnen

Voorhout

S

De Klei

N206

WIJK
N ZEE

A44

Warmond

Katwijk a/d Rijn

Rijnsburg

Notes:

Notes:

FARM TOURS
FLOWERPICKINGGARDENS

Cheese Farm De Annahoeve Menneweg 42 2172 HE Sassenheim
Tel. 0252 - 213 018 www.deannahoeve.nl

FAM Flower Farm Heereweg 361 2161 CB Lisse
Tel. 0252 - 211 462 www.famflowerfarm.nl

Flower Farm De Tulperij Oude Herenweg 16B 2215 RZ Voorhout
Tel. 0252 - 228 720 www.detulperij.nl

Annemieke's Picking Garden Haarlemmerstraat 15a 2182 HA Hillegom
Tel. 06 - 53 83 99 79 www.annemiekespluktuin.nl

De Bollenburcht Teylingerlaan 13 2215 RT Voorhout
Tel. 0252 - 225 031 www.bollenburcht.nl

ELECTRIC CAR GPS TOURS